Spinning Wheel's

Collectible Iron, Tin, Copper & Brass

𝔖𝔭𝔦𝔫𝔫𝔦𝔫𝔤 𝔚𝔥𝔢𝔢𝔩'𝔰
Collectible Iron, Tin, Copper & Brass

edited by
Albert Christian Revi

CASTLE BOOKS

Copyright © 1974 Spinning Wheel Magazine, Everybodys Press, Inc.

Published Under Arrangement With Ottenheimer Publishers, Inc.
Printed in the United States of America

Introduction

Suprisingly, metalwares of all kinds have appealed to both men and women. Objects of iron, brass, copper and tin have been fashioned in simple and very sophisticated designs; their uses were often utilitarian, but some of the most decorative designs have been lavished on even the meanest objects.

Realizing the universal appeal of metalwares, simple and elaborate, the Editors of *Spinning Wheel* have met collectors' needs by publishing authoritative articles by well-known authors, collectors, and museum curators. This book is a compilation of selected articles about iron, brass, copper, and tinwares. More than that, it represents the very best information available on these subjects.

Iron, brass, and copper were known to the ancient Egyptians; they were used throughout the early eastern and western cultures, including China. Tinwares are, by comparison, somewhat late arrivals. But the production of tinware became widespread soon after its introduction, and more particularly in the late 17th and early 18th centuries.

For some years before the Revolution, American colonists depended on England for most of their metalwares—especially brass, copper and tinware. Soon the colonials were establishing their own metalworking shops and dependence on England for such supplies diminished rapidly. While metalware shops sprung up here and there throughout the colonies, there appears to have been more produced in Pennsylvania, based on the preponderance of signed examples extant. Even so, brass, copper and tinware continued to be imported from England and France as late as 1890. The sophistication of European designs was preferred to the less elaborate productions made in America. Since this was the case, we have covered all metalwares, both domestic and imported, in this book.

Albert Christian Revi, Editor
Spinning Wheel
Hanover, Penna. 17331

Table of Contents

18th Century Iron Furnaces

by HENRY J.
KAUFFMAN

Fireback for woodburning fireplace. Photo courtesy Metropolitan Museum of Art.

THE pre-eminent position of Pennsylvania in the modern world of iron and steel is well known and all people quickly recognize names as Bethlehem, Lukens, Midvale, Carnegie, Laughlin and Jones, but only those who have made a study of eighteenth century iron making in Pennsylvania are familiar with names such as Durham, Warwick, Elizabeth, Hopewell, Cornwall, Martic, Mary Ann and others. Despite the importance of the early iron industry in Pennsylvania, it should be pointed out that the industry did not have its beginning here for the first recorded attempt to build a furnace occurred at Falling Creek, Virginia, but it was doomed to sudden failure because of an Indian massacre when all the buildings were destroyed before iron could be produced. The first successful establishment occured at Saugus Center near Lynn, Massachusetts in 1685, sixty-four years after the Virginia attempt. Massachusetts can claim another seventeenth century furnace and numerous eighteenth century ones, but from the standpoint of numbers and importance of their products Pennsylvania had more eighteenth century furnaces than any of the colonial areas.

The reason for the location of the furnaces is very easy to explain, for Pennsylvania was particularly blessed with the raw products to produce the iron. In the first place there was an abundance of ore, particularly in the Lancaster, Lebanon, Berks, and Chester County areas, some of which is being mined today at Cornwall. The old furnace at Cornwall is in an excellent state of preservation and is a historical shrine under the control of the Historical Commission of Pennsylvania, but its adjacent ore pit continues to produce a rich grade of iron ore and has been worked constantly from the day of its opening in 1742. It is one of the most important sources of magnetite ore in America and due to its proximity to the surface much of it can be loaded by shovels into trucks and conveyed to the crusher. Copper, silver, and gold are among the important by-products secured from the mine. Most of the other mining

Iron master's house at Hopewell Village. Kauffman photo.

areas have fallen before the importance of the great sources in the Great Lake region and with the exception of the Cornwall area most of the eighteenth century iron producing areas have attained a museum status.

In addition to ore, a fuel was required to produce iron and Pennsylvania was particularly endowed with an abundance of virgin growth. The farmers of the Palatinate were attracted to Pennsylvania by the stories of the rich river valleys and walnut trees, but it was the beech, black oak, ash and white oak that attracted the iron masters. Beech was regarded as the best for charcoal and much must have fallen before the axes of the skilled European woodchoppers. It was chopped to length, skillfully piled in a tapering shape like a tepee and then covered with mud. A smoldering fire was nurtured until the wood had turned to charcoal, the operation requiring constant attendance for if the fire secured draft and broke through the mud the entire pile would quickly be consumed by flames. A small opening was allowed at the top which provided a place to start the fire and a source of a bit of oxygen to keep it smoldering. It was imperative that an adequate supply of woodland adjoin each furnace and the woodland was included whenever deals effecting the transfer of the furnace occurred.

The problem of iron making was further solved in Pennsylvania with the presence of incalcuable quantities of limestone for flux. Poured into the top of the furnace in well regulated ratios with the ore and the charcoal the limestone was always needed to make the operation a successful one. Limestone was a willing slave of the iron master for he not only used it for its chemical properties, but it is possible that the furnace itself may have been built of it and lined with a more fire-resisting brick or slate. His residence could also have been built of the same material and Southeastern Pennsylvania can still point to a few eighteenth century homes that have not fallen to the axe of fashion or modernization.

There was also a need for skilled craftsmen to build furnaces and homes and despite the fact that most of the furnace owners were Englishmen it is not likely that they allowed the skill of the German immigrants to go unnoticed. Several industries in England were developed by German skill, such as textiles, copper and brass, and it is likely that the Germans had quite a hand in Pennsylvania where their mechanical skill could supplement English capital. A great deal was required beyond the furnace, for in addition a dam had to be built, runways to the furnace constructed and water wheels as big as twenty-five feet in diameter had to be constructed and installed. These wheels tripped the ends of a huge bellows thereby creating the cold blast that was required for high temperature and the fusing of the ore. Later the bellows were replaced by pressure tubs and the water wheels were replaced by steam power in some furnaces while other furnaces became obsolete and closed before any renovations were made.

It becomes obvious that the details of running a furnace required a complete and almost self sustaining village and in Hopewell Village near Reading, Pennsylvania, it is known that a small group including woodchoppers, colliers, teamsters, blacksmiths, moulders, and wheelwrights lived in the shadow of the big house on the hill where the iron master lived. It is also possible that this group would include cabinetmakers, cordwainers, coverlet weavers, carpenters, and perhaps a wood carver or a pattern maker to supply patterns for the stove plates or other products of the furnace.

The sociological aspect of this small village appear rather depressing for it is likely that all these people lived in what is known today as "company" houses, they traded at a "company" store, and their entire economy was regulated by a scale that was very unlikely to favor the worker. The workers' lot was considerably improved over his Earlier European status, but it must have been mostly on the mental side for his greatest advance was in the little likelihood of war and pillaging.

Beyond these skilled and semi-skilled groups lived another group of which not much is known but records frequently refer to the slaves and indentured servants that were connected with the furnace. By 1722 indentured servants were arriving at the port of Philadelphia in great numbers who were sold at 10 pounds each to serve a period of three or four years. In addition there were Negro slaves and Indian laborers who received nothing but the barest necessities for anything beyond that which would have permitted them to save and flee their master thereby causing endless trouble, as was sometimes the case.

Recently a number of meagerly marked graves have been found which appear to be the graves of obscure workers at the Martic Fur-

nace. In a patch that is completely covered with undergrowth the small gravestones are almost completely lost because of lack of interest and loss of identity of the occupants. Such is the fate of the workers, but the monuments of the iron masters are huge stone houses with bronze plaques enumerating their contributions to humanity.

The eighteenth century furnaces were comparable to two distinct units in todays industrial production. They were first and essentially furnaces producing iron, frequently pig iron which was then moved to a forge and by the use of water power and a large hammer the pigs were reduced to a size that was useful to the local blacksmith for making articles of wrought iron. Secondly, they were also foundries for before the furnace and under a roof lay a large area of sand with flasks where the cast articles of the day were made. Among the articles were mortars, betty lamps, kettles, cannon, pots, frying pans, tea-kettles, cannon balls, other hollow ware, stoves, firebacks, and stove plates.

Little remains of the products of the eighteenth century iron furnace for the twentieth century collector, but the one item which is available is most intriguing, although it is a bit cumbersome to collect——stove plates. These parts of five-plate stoves like much other Americana were left to rust and disintegrate until interest was aroused in them. Then they came to be regarded as one of the choice possessions of the Pennsylvania Germans and only they appear to have used them in America. Reminiscent of their European prototypes the German natives of Pennsylvania demanded that the English furnace owners supply their wants and produce a stove similar to the ones they had used in their homeland.

The stoves consisted of five plates, bolted together, two sides, a top and bottom, and one end, thereby leaving an aperture which was inserted in a wall opposite a fire place in an adjoining room. The wide space on the edge of the plate illustrated permitted the stove to be inserted into the plaster of the wall, without imparing the completeness of the design. The end opposite the wide space or the front end of the stove was supported by bricks or some sort of fired earthenware which would not mar the floor, or conduct heat too readily. The stove was fired from the fireplace of the next room which also provided a chimney for the exit of the smoke. These were known as non-ventilating stoves and had no opening into the room which they heated.

No mystery surrounds the origin of the stove for it is definitely known that the Pennsylvania plates had European ancestors which were used throughout Germany and Scandinavia. The English never used stoves at this time but resorted to the use of open fireplaces such as the ones used when New England was settled. It is not known if the first Amerrican plates were cast from European plates or from wooden patterns, for many European plates were brought to America, some bearing dates that antedate any casting activity here. Most early plates, the first American one being 1726, consisted of two areas with a horizontal line going through the center of the plates. Above the line was a biblical scene such as the Delilah and Samson plate illustrated or numerous other motifs such as The Temptation of Joseph, Abraham and Isaac, Susanna and the Elders, Adam and Eve, Mary and Martha, and David and Jonathan. In some cases these motifs were presumed to be copied from the wood cut illustrations of a German Bible or in most cases were the artists interpretation of the text below. The text in the lower part of the early plate was usually in German and explained the motif at the top. The plate of the later six-plate stove had a conventionalized flower motif in the top part, and the bottom portion bearing the name of the iron master such as H. Wilhelm Stiegel, who also added Elizabeth Furnace or more frequently only the date indicating the time that the plate was cast. Most of the dated plates occur from 1760 to 1770.

The six-plate stove followed the five-plate stove and differed chiefly in the respect that it was moved away from the wall and had a stove pipe for ventilating, plus an cpen-ing in the front or side plate to insert wood and remove ashes. It frequently stood on cast iron legs and slightly resembled the later ten-plate stoves which are sometimes found in Pennsylvania kitchens today. Hopewell Furnace is known to have made plates for six-plate stoves but due to its late establishment (about 1760), and the fact that the art of stove plate making was in the decline, the well known example bearing the name of the iron master Mark Bird with that of Hopewell and 1772, the plate shows little of the earlier art in its decadent flower motif.

Although one plate pattern of wood is extant today there seems to be little doubt that patterns for all the plates existed and by some curious turn of events nearly all have been destroyed. These patterns were pressed in the sand in front of the furnace and when the furnace was tapped the molten iron flowed in shallow gutters to each opening, the entrance being closed when the shallow pit was filled. This technique accounts for the rough texture on the back of all plates and for the slight discrepancies in the thickness.

Similar to stove plates and often confused with them are the firebacks which were formed in the same manner as the stove plates and in Pennsylvania often bore similar decorative motifs. Due to the early establishments of furnaces and the frequent use of the backs by the English, it is presumed by some authorities that some firebacks were cast in New England prior to 1720 when Cole Brook Dale Furnace was started in Pennsylvania. They bear no relation to the stove which they slightly resemble but were used exclusively for decorative purposes and for reflecting heat in the back of wood burning fireplaces. They were continued in use beyond the time of the five and six plate stoves and were probably used throughout the colonies wherever there were English residents and there was a need for a fireplace.

The specimen illustrated has a sun with divergent rays in the area above the motif, in the center is the band indicating the name of the furnace.

A cast iron five-plate stove, dated 1760, with Biblical quotation "Las Dich Nicht Gelyssten Deines Neststen Gut" (Thou shalt not covet they neighbor's goods).

Early American Stove Plates

by LESTER BREININGER, JR.

A STOVE PLATE is a side, actually a section, of a jamb stove, more commonly called a five-plate stove. Numerous mid-18th century Germanic houses in America had a large, centrally located fireplace. A "hole" in

This fine stove plate, along with its side partners, front plate, and bottom plate, were covering the chimney of a spring house until they appeared at a farm sale in Pennsylvania in the spring of 1971. It appears to depict the Biblical story of the five wise virgins who trimmed their lamps and awaited the arrival of the bridegroom. Collection Lee Leister.

the back opened into a rear or side room, normally a parlor-type room. Projecting into this room from the back of the fireplace was an iron box consisting of five sand cast iron plates. These were bolted together and rested on a square cut stone or a brick column on the floor.

This arrangement, in essence, acted like a radiator. Logs burning in the

fireplace or in the stove itself would heat the room with no dirt caused by wood being carried, ashes removed, or even, hopefully, from escaping smoke.

The top and bottom plates of this stove were usually of plain iron. The front and sides were quite often decorated. Designs of arches with tulips and hearts abounded. Others were religiously inspired. Verses from scripture often accompanied by vivid portrayals of Biblical events (i.e. The Lord's Supper, the Wedding at Cana, and Adam and Eve) were quite popular. One of these plates admonishes "Las Dich Nicht Gelyssten Dienes Heststen Gut" (Thou shalt not covet . . .). The name Wilhelm

A badly rusted example showing four figures at table, one at the top of the stairs, and one drawing wine from a jug. The inscription states, "The first sign Christ 'did,' turned the water into wine, John the second chapter."

A fine example of "Dutch" embellishment, dated 1760. Courtesy Historical Society of Berks County.

Bortschend (William Bird shines) also appears on it. The word "shines" probably refers to his exceptional ability to produce such decorative plates. Bird was an ironmaster of Berks County who died about 1760.

Probably the most collectible stove plates were made by Henry W. Stiegel, colonial ironmaster and glassmaker of the Lancaster County Elizabeth Furnace. The subsequent invention, attributed to him, of the ten plate stove in 1765 (a self contained stove with an iron base, stovepipe and oven) dealt a death blow to the fancy, decorative stove plates.

With the demand gone, artistry withered. Though James Old of Chester County Reading Furnace, among others, was still producing stove plates in 1786, they are usually quite unimpressive and were evidently merely replacement parts of jamb stoves still in use in the older homes.

As the use of these stove plates was discontinued, the plates were put to other uses. Some were just set against the back of the fireplace. This practice is still so common, even among antiques collectors, that a goodly number of persons think these plates were originally made as fire backs. Many plates were used as elevated platforms for fires in smoke house, wash house and other outbuildings; some appeared as stepping stones; others were placed under rain spouts to prevent washing; and still others were scrapped.

While a visit to the Mercer Museum in Doylestown would convince most people that all the stove plates in existence are in that collection, some plates still become available to collectors. (See The Bible in Iron, by Dr. Henry C. Mercer, happily, again in print.)

An excellent stove plate dated 1742 turned up last year at a public sale. It had been used as the base of an ash pile in a cellar fireplace. Fortunately, it was face down and the fires had not obliterated the design. More recently one was discovered at a Berks County farmhouse. In winter it was propped against the cellar window, in summer merely moved against the solid cellar wall.

Like gold, stove plates are where you find them. A piece of iron sticking out of a mud bank interested a muskrat trapper who proceeded to discover a stove plate; only one-fourth protruded, but it was sufficient to catch his attention. While an old outdoor bake oven was being torn down to make room for a garage, another stove plate appeared. Another was merely set against a smoke house about four inches deep in mud. Others have literally gone to pieces while serving as stepping stones.

Probably the best find was at the Sweitzer home in Brecknock Township, Berks County. While remodeling his ancient dwelling in 1907, a jamb stove was torn out to be eventually discarded. This stove was acquired by the Historical Society of Berks County (Reading, Pa.) in 1909 and is now on display there. This is one of the few original plate jamb stoves in existence. However, the original bolts and fastenings had been discarded. Most stoves in museum collections are composite ones.

One of the most distressing things to a stove plate collector's heart is the kind of information found in a ledger from Charming Forge. A bar iron forge in Berks County, once owned by the

Iron Stove plate depicting "The Flight Into Egypt"; ca. 1755. Courtesy Historical Society of Berks County.

legendary "Baron" Stiegel, it operated from 1750 to 1886. From an account of 1843 it disposed to one F. Sellers, in January of that year:

Old Stove Plates

Tons	Cwt.	Quarters	Lbs.
2	15	1	17
6	0	21	

(The hauling credited to his account at .75/Ton.)

Undoubtedly other people besides Mr. Sellers found a profit in reclaiming these old stove plates. The scrap drives of World War II took an additional toll of the remaining stove plates.

They are getting scarce nowadays, but because they are quite large, 21 x 23 inches being a common size, heavy, 70-90 pounds, and cumbersome, they are not enjoying the popularity of some other collectibles. Collectors who do have them, besides using them as decorative fire backs, often frame and mount them on the wall in the hallway, entranceway, or stairway. As early examples of our country's resourcefulness, artistry, and skill in metal working, they deserve a greater interest in their study and preservation.

Collecting Cast Iron Comfort

by FLORENCE THOMPSON HOWE

Cast-iron comfort with an old wood-burning Victorian stove of elegant design.

OLD STOVES, in today's electrically operated space-age, are fast becoming as obsolete as the horse and buggy or the milkman. Should world conditions create an oil shortage, as was the case in the second World War in the early 1940s, these old wood-burning stoves could become the pot of gold at the end of the heatless householder's rainbow.

Hopefully, no such situation will arise. But these antique heat makers still have a place, even in the normal programs of the "affluent society." There's cast iron comfort for you in the old wood-burning stove in a hunting cabin or a fishing shack; in a guest cottage or studio at your summer place; or even in the ell of a remodelled farmhouse in a cold climate. Installed as stand-by equipment, they do a job for you in remote areas where electricity suffers frequent "outages" from storms. They'll keep your water pipes from freezing or, used as auxiliary heat, cut your operating cost on your main heating system in extreme weather.

But where could you buy a stove today? Not at a city hardware store. At the antique dealer's, the second-hand shop, or the country auction, perhaps. So it's good to know something about these old stoves before you buy.

Philadelphia pattern stoves were introduced in New England in the

Wood-burner with Gothic facade and dainty cabriole legs made in Troy, N. Y.

PHILIP WILLCOX,

Has received an additional supply of

Cooking

AND

Open

STOVES

which with his former stock makes his
assortment as extensive and complete as
can be found at any store in the county.
The above Stoves he *does not sell on
commission* but *buys* them for CASH at
VERY REDUCED PRICES, which enables
him to sell them *lower* than they can be
bought at any commission store in this
town.

STOVE
PIPE,

all sizes, constantly on
hand in any quantity.
New FIXTURES
made to old stoves,
and all other work in
his line of business furnished at short
notice.

Also, will be kept constantly on
on hand a large and complete assortment of IRON HOLLOW WARE,
at low prices.

Purchasers are respectfully invited
to call before they buy, at the Brick
Store, one door west of the Bank, State
street, where they may exchange most
kinds of *Country Produce*, CASH, or
good credit, to the best advantage, for
any of the above articles

Springfield Dec 15   6771

In 1827, Phillip Wilcox advertised stoves,
stove pipes, and iron hollow ware.

early 1800s, some of them are dated
"1774." Stumble onto one of these
and you really have a collector's item.
They were box stoves with an oven
over the fire. The only boiler hose
was in the bottom of the oven. Castings weighed from 700 to 800 pounds
and appeared to have been made by
pouring the metal into an open flat
mold. There was no rim on the pipe-
hole by which to secure the pipe, but
a wrought-iron rim of a half-inch.

thickness with a flange for support
was fitted to the hole to form the
union between the stove and the pipe.

A Philip Willcox stove is worth
picking up, too. Philip Willcox was a
stove-maker and an early merchant
(1823) in Springfield, Massachusetts.

Wood-burning stove with hearth and brass
finials on top made by Philip Wilcox. First
quarter 19th century.

The "Economy" wood and coal heating and
cooking stove manufactured by Comstock,
Castle & Co., Quincy, Ill., ca. 1880.

Wood-burning stove of sheet metal bears manufacturer's identification "Reeves/Dover/ Copper Alloy."

He thought well of his merchandise, for in one of his advertisements he says:

PHILIP WILLCOX

Respectfully informs his friends and the public that he has just received from New York an assortment of E. Hoyt's highly approved patent COOKING STOVES. The above mentioned stoves are so constructed as to convey the steam arising from the boilers (which is admitted to be almost the only objection to cooking stoves) directly into the pipe without the least inconvenience to the cooking; also the extreme heat that arises directly from the fire passes off, which renders it equally as pleasant and as healthy as an open Franklin; with the addition of his patent oven. They are considered by those who have had them in use, superior to any stoves offered to the public.

Willcox also advertised in 1826, stove-pipes, live geese feathers, and fan and side lights, probably for the old front door, "filled to any pattern." He announced, too, that "PEDLARS will be accommodated with a good

assortment, and at low prices." And believe it or not, he said he had "a bathing-tub to let."

Styles and decorative design in 19th century stoves usually related to the furniture of the period. Delicate Victorian filigree often reflected a mighty hot fire. There were some of the New York-born "parlor" stoves that were positively Gothic in feeling. Others, notably those made by the Shakers in Connecticut, were chaste and simple, with ornamentation reduced to the least common denominator. These little Shaker stoves, low-slung, long and narrow, with duck feet, would not be out of tune with contemporary decor.

The Franklin stoves used often today in lieu of fire-place heating, carry much of fireplace charm, but throw out more heat because not so much is lost up the chimney. Franklin himself said of his device: "My common room, I know, is made twice as warm as it used to be with a quarter of the

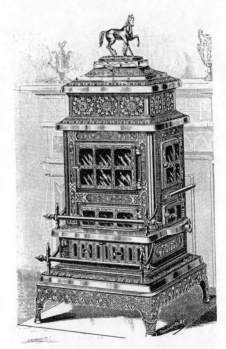

"The Ivy," manufactured by The Richmond Stove Co., Norwich, Conn., 1882. Decorated with Low's Art Tiles, bronze and nickel trimmings.

wood I formerly consumed there."
(This he wrote in 1744!)

Antiques dealers report that there is still much interest in these old stoves. Prices vary, of course, with their age, condition, and desirability either for functional use or decorative antiques. One of the most delightful of the later stoves is an early model of the Florence oilstove, a rococo little number topped with a slide-out plate and grill. Called "Florence Favorite," and dated "1871," it is only 18 inches high. It is not a wood-burner, but it throws out a lot of heat on a gallon of oil! A forerunner, doubtless, of our present-day portable, though much more engaging in appearance, it is really a desirable old stove. It was made by the Florence Mfg. Co. of Florence, Massachusetts, almost a hundred years ago.

Early oilstove (1871) made by Florence Manufacturing Co., Florence, Mass.; height 18 inches.

Universal Base Burner No. 50, manufactured by Co-Operative Stove Works, Troy, N. Y., 1883.

Beauty in Wrought Iron

Some Pictures and Notes Concerning Items Well Worth Collecting and Using.

Sugar Auger. An item of utilitarian beauty of the sort that was all in the day's work for our accomplished ironsmiths, or blacksmiths. Most of us think of black-smiths in terms of our own memory; as horseshoers. But it was this type of artisan who made all the beautiful wrought iron of our early days.

by CARL DREPPERD

THE first iron wrought in what is now our country was mined and melted at Saugus, Massachusetts, early in the 17th century. It was bog iron, "mined" by dredging out the lumps of almost pure ore in neighboring bogs, mires and fenns. Not until the rich deposits of Penn's colony were opened by Cornish and Welsh ironmasters did iron become a staple of Colonial manufacture. In fact, so great were the deposits of Pennsylvania and so active the production that England put an embargo on it; it couldn't be shipped to England in exchange for other goods. Not until the great western deposits in the Great Lakes region were discovered did the Grubb mines in upper Lancaster County yield the palm for American ore production.

Ironsmiths "ironed" a house by making everything that went into its building, including the hardware, the shutter holdbacks, snow birds, beam heads, H and HL hinges, rat tail hinges and foot scrapers, latches, lifts, locks and keys. These men also wrought cabinet hardware, and innumerable other items. For example, look at that beautiful three pronged, curling, screw which originally had a cross-handle of wood. What is it? The piece is beautiful because it is a perfect tool for its use. It is a **sugar auger.** When sugar was made in the old fashioned way, syrup was crystallized and poured into cone shaped molds for small packages of up to 40 pounds, and in barrels containing up to 250 pounds.

These molds, and barrels, were drained as the solid sugar formed, the drainage being "syrup" or molasses. Then, when ready for market, the sugar was as hard as a bone. You had

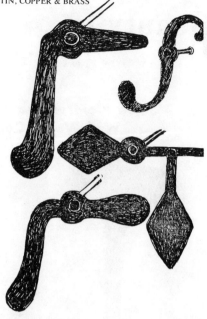

Foot scrapers. The two top ones are of the type that were driven in a wood step tread, or set in stone treads, anchored in lead. At center, a scraper to attach to the side of step, level with tread. Bottom, a scraper set aside of step riser, or at a wall corner.

Shutter Holdbacks. Top, the Swan's Head, and the "S" types, noted used from Queen Anne Period. Bottom, Later, and simpler forms, used to the 1850's, but noted on many mid to late 18th century town and country houses.

to gouge it out of barrels, loosening it . . . and so, the sugar auger was devised. The cones were not augered. They were formed with a hanging cord in them, and were cut apart with (1) Sugar cleavers and (2) Sugar nippers.

Pictured also are some excellent examples of wrought iron as used in home building, all of which are explained in the captions. This little essay is an introduction to "old wrought iron" which we have had in mind for some time. In fact several friends of ours have undertaken the compilation of a monograph on old iron which would show most of the available kinds and sorts of pieces known to have been made from the late 1680's right through to the 1880's. So if you want more on this subject, please let your wishes be known by the simple expedient of dropping us a postal card. We hope a thousand of our many thousands of readers will want more about this most fascinating category of collecting and an item of antiquity that is bound to increase in interest, and in value, down through the years.

The Charm
of Cast Iron

by HENRY J. KAUFFMAN

Heart-shaped waffle iron thought to be 18th century and of Pennsylvania origin.

Unmarked mortar and pestle. Many of these were made in America in the 19th century. Only a few bear the imprint of the maker. Kauffman Collection.

THE COLLECTING cognoscenti, whose specialty has been the artifacts of the 17th and 18th centuries are now turning to those of more recent origin. The products of Paul Revere, Henry Will, and Thomas Savery seem to have vanished, and what was once regarded as nondescript is now moving slowly to the center of the stage.

The logical solution for the embryonic collector is to begin acquiring commodities which have been back stage or are just emerging from the wings to show up in recent antiques shows and prestigious shops. Objects made of cast iron fit into this category; some early trivets and Hessian soldier and andirons are now regarded as good company for objects made of silver, pewter, or blown glass.

A limitation inherent in objects made of cast iron is that the material itself cannot claim an ancient heritage. None was found in the tomb of King Tutankhamen, nor did the Greeks use it in building the Parthenon. Cast iron is an invention of the late Middle

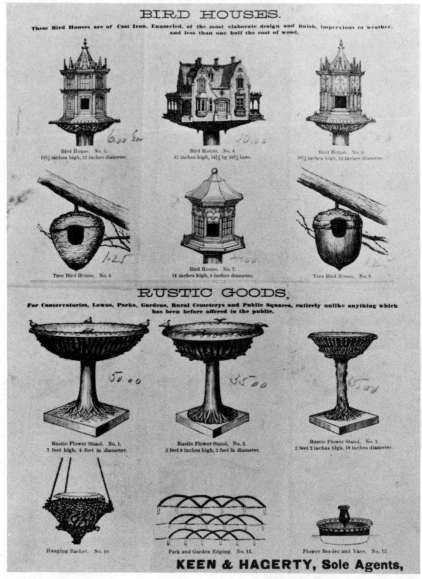

Bird houses and "Rustic" goods made of cast iron were sold by Keen & Hagerty of Baltimore, Md., in the late 19th century.

Ages and a virtual newcomer among the substances of which important objects are made. If a blob of cast iron did appear in a bloomery before that time, it was thrown away because technicians did not know what to do with it.

By American standards, however, it is old, almost as old as the earliest settlements, for in the 1640s a furnace was built at Saugus, Massachusetts. It has recently been rebuilt so that anyone who visits it may see how metal was cast "in the good old days." Incidentally, Saugus was the first capitalistic venture in the New World, a fact which has little relevance to its production of artifacts. Up to now, only one product remains which can be attributed to it with any degree of confidence, but as objects of cast iron become increasingly sought after, others may be found.

Throughout the 18th and 19th centuries, many furnaces were operating along the eastern seacoast, producing pigs of iron as well as numerous finished objects such as cannons, cannon balls, skillets, griddles, trivets, kettles, firebacks, stove parts, and mortars and pestles. Over the years, most of these products had been relegated to scrap heaps or the bottoms of wells. Some of them have been rescued and given places of prominence in private collections and museums. Unfortunately,

Waffle iron of cast iron decorated with Pennsylvania German motifs. Kauffman Collection.

Trivet of cast iron marked on the back "W. B. Rimby, Baltimore, 1843." Notice the use of Pennsylvania German decorative motifs. Osburn Collection.

Tulips decorate this cast iron trivet. Marked on the back "W. B. R. 1843." The flat surfaces on the designs were created by wear, probably sliding of a flat-iron across its surface for many years.

Three-legged iron kettle with the name of the maker, Sampson and Tisdale, cast into its side. This firm was listed as "foundrymen" in New York City in the first half of the 19th century. Kauffman Collection.

only a few of these fascinating objects can be identified as the products of a particular furnace or foundry since the name of the facility which produced them was rarely imprinted by the pattern maker or foundryman.

Possibly the most desirable products of the furnace in the collector's view are firebacks and stove plates. To make these, patterns of wood were pressed in a bed of sand in front of a furnace; after the furnace was tapped, the cavity was filled with molten iron. In this way the details of the pattern were dramatically duplicated.

A fireback was a single sheet of iron placed against the back wall of the fireplace to promote the reflection of heat into the room, a function for which a masonry wall was quite ineffective. Before the 1760s, when stove pipe came into common use in America, a Pennsylvania stove consisted of five plates, the open end being inserted into the rear wall of a fireplace in the adjoining room. The wood was fed into the stove through the fireplace, and both the stove and the fireplace used a common chimney for the disposal of smoke. Many of the side plates of the stoves were decorated with designs with Biblical themes. An authoritative book, describing these

stove plates in great detail, was published in 1914 by their most avid collector, Henry Mercer. It is aptly called *The Bible In Iron*.

Several furnaces were famous because they produced military "materiel" for the American Revolution, but such products are a bit clumsy to collect, and few of them have survived. A cannon which was rejected because of imperfections lies on the casting bed at Cornwall Furnace, near Lebanon, Pennsylvania. Such identification is unusual. In general the lack of identifying marks has caused a certain apathy among collectors regarding the owning of such objects.

A number of so-called gypsy kettles survive, ranging in size from quite small to very large, which bear the names of the furnaces where they were cast. Although the large kettles cannot be regarded as household collectibles, the small ones fit well into this category; a perfect example might be regarded by some collectors as an object of considerable charm. In addition, a number of signed teakettles survive; these are attractive, particularly if they are suspended with a tilting device, which permits the pouring of hot

Cast iron facade on a building at Front and Arch Streets, Philadelphia, Pa. It is reported that the front on a nearby building is hinged so that the entire facade can be swung outward.

water from the kettle without removing it from the fireplace.

A profusion of trivets has survived; however, most of them might be regarded as "late," and few of the earliest examples are signed. W. B. Rimby, a foundryman working in Baltimore in the 1840s, made several attractive models, some of which are signed and dated. Doubtless other signed examples survive; however, those by Rimby are particularly pleasing. His use of Pennsylvania folk art motifs suggests that many of them were made for merchants or peddlers operating in Pennsylvania.

Frying pans, andirons, mortars and pestles, and similar objects frequently bear the imprint of their makers. Some

Cast iron tea kettle marked "I. Savery, New York." An 1842 business directory for New York City listed J. Savery and Son (William) as merchants located at 113 Beekman Street. Shelburne Museum Collection.

of the cast iron balusters and porch posts used in the South were made in the North and shipped to such ports as Charleston and New Orleans. When the gold rush was at its height, entire houses of cast iron were shipped to California where they were assembled in a few days; they proved to be completely adequate for miners who were "in a hurry."

Finally, in the middle of the 19th century, entire buildings were constructed of cast iron, some of them being many stories high. The most famous structure was the Crystal Palace in London which housed the great British Trade Exhibition of 1851. A few buildings in America employed a facade of cast iron. A number of them survive in the Front and Arch Street area in Philadelphia. Though one can collect such items only photographically, they remain an interesting facet of American industry and architecture and are well worth preserving as typical of an era when America was solidly built.

Friends of Cast-Iron Architecture

The Friends of Cast-Iron Architecture are seeking new members who want to see that cast-iron buildings are recognized and appreciated. Honorary co-chairmen of the group are Henry-Russell Hitchcock and Sir Nikolaus Pevsner. Dues for becoming a Friend are $2.00. Write: Mrs. Margot Gayle, Chairman, Friends of Cast-Iron Architecture, 44 West 9th Street, Room 20, New York, N.Y. 10011.

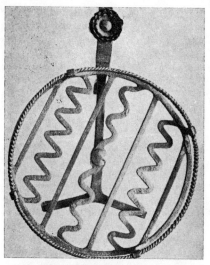

Handwrought Iron Trivets

by DICK HANKENSON

HANDWROUGHT iron trivets of the eighteenth and early nineteenth centuries — and a few were known to be in use in America as early as the seventeenth—stood in the fireplace or on the hearth to hold a pot or kettle whose contents were to be kept warm. They were of all sizes and shapes — triangular, round, rectangular, even of irregular design. They were made with high legs and short legs — the high-legged trivets were the earliest type—with handles, and without handles. Some were made at home by the man of the house; most were fashioned by the village blacksmith. Either the housewife suggested a design for her trivet, or the blacksmith followed his own ideas. No two are found exactly alike.

Many methods of decoration were used. In some cases, metal was heated in the forge, bent into shapes and twisted for artistic decoration. Trivets are found with inserts of iron, or even copper, cut in fancy shapes. Sometimes these inserts were hammered attractively.

Trivet legs and feet were often very fancy. Some were twisted and flattened; more were welded to the body

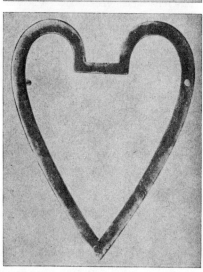

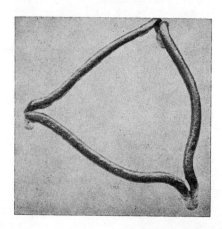

ILLUSTRATIONS

Counterclockwise from top:

Rare Lazy Susan with unusual railing of twisted iron. Body is of forged pieces welded together; side supports for railing are riveted to body, bent over railing. Legs are forged and bent, welded together; short handle has applied 3-piece rosette. Large loose rivet allows turning.

The rim here is a flat iron strip; center bars and legs are each one piece, riveted to rim.

Early "Heart" design; body forged of one piece and welded at point; legs riveted to body.

Forged of round iron, three separate pieces are used, with legs bent down. All pieces forge-welded together.

Intricate detail is shown here; crossbars are mortised into body, legs bent down, rattail handle used. Design is hand-cut with cold chisel.

Three separate pieces of square iron are forge-welded together; legs and body are formed of the same pieces.

by the forge-welding process. In this, the metal was heated in the forge to a very high temperature; a little flux was added; and the two pieces of metal were joined by hammering them together on the anvil.

Occasionally trivets were found with the legs riveted on. Here, a hole was made in the edge of the body, the shaped leg inserted, and the protruding end pounded until it was riveted tight. This method was also used when an insert was added as part of the body.

Handles were frequently ornate, and disclosed a fine quality of workmanship. Rattail ends were made by heating the iron and drawing the metal to a point by hammer and anvil.

Wrought iron stands for smoothing irons, also called trivets, were in early use. They are most often found in triangular shape, though they were made in other shapes, too. About 1830 cast iron trivets appeared, and by 1850, the handwrought iron trivet was well on its way to oblivion.

Wrought iron trivets, pictured, from the author's collection, indicate various types and shapes that may be found, and should be cherished.

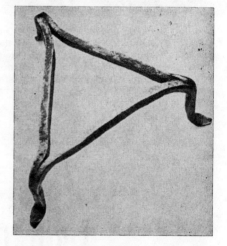

Left, top row: Star and leaf form from a Dutch smoothing board; Heart and keys with Ying-yeng or Chinese Swastika center, scalloped edge; Star and circles, with openwork saw edge. **Bottom row:** Star and hearts, openwork, ribbed border. Note the pointed oval separating heart at the bottom. This clue would seem to indicate the design is lifted from a Dutch carved spoon rack; Star and loops; with open saw edge; Star and circles with scalloped edge. None of these trivets have handles. They range in size from four to eight inches in diameter. All are cast iron.

Cast and Wrought Iron Trivets

by HUGO DARMSTAETTER

THE sheer and unalloyed pleasures that lurk in collecting little things in the field of antiques is a discovery which, perhaps, every collector must make for himself. While it is quite true that my own collecting habits and activities are in the field of furniture, the birth of my collecting and its continuation is due to my mother who, in some twenty years, collected over seven hundred, all different, cast and wrought iron trivets or stands. Her collection, while of little things, is on the heavy side. Yet I have been told by more than one decorator of note that this collection, accumulated piece by piece, would make a series of most interesting interior walls by mounting the trivets against an oyster-white background.

The cast trivet for flatirons was made in so many different designs by so many large and small ironfounders from the early 1800s down to the early 1900s that the total production must have reached an astounding figure. In the research thus far conducted, it would seem that every iron foundry of record, at some time or other in its history, cast a number of these objects, either as original designs by their own pattern makers or as copies of trivets made by some other foundry. It has been said that if a foundry cast stoves, grates or parts, it also cast trivets. With this production established, in theory at least, who can say it is only theory when we view the infinite number of trivets that have survived the years? To say the total production was a million a year for a hundred years might even be an understatement. Yet now these trivets are getting scarce, and some of the really early examples are quite rare. We may even agree that the term unique, or one-of-a-kind, can be applied to certain examples.

It would seem a rather hopeless task to attempt a tabulation of what foundries made what trivets, and when. Very few of them are marked except those designed as advertisements for the foundries. Often a stove works supplied each distributor or retailer with hundreds of trivets, to be passed out as advertisements for the stove, and as gifts to buyers of stoves. These trivets, generally, are marked and carry the name or some insignia of the foundry. But many really lovely trivets are unmarked. The same thing is true of the wrought iron trivets which, generally earlier than the cast iron ones, were the individual work of artisans at the forge. It goes without saying that every wrought iron trivet is an individual production and that even though it may have been made over and over again as a type, it is doubtful if any two so made, even by the same smith, are precisely alike. The temptation to vary the designs, if ever so slightly, while hammering and welding thin straps of iron, generally caused the worker to add his own individual touch.

But since these trivets do exist in numbers that puts them within the realm of deserved classification, it is quite logical that an attempt be made at such classification, using the facilities of one of the larger collections to start with. Since I have fallen heir to such a collection I have, tentatively at least, the fol-

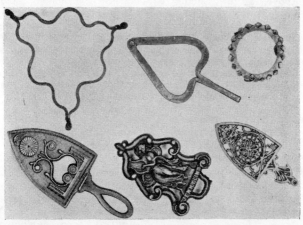

Above, top: Wrought iron Triangle form trivet with flat button feet; Spade, or heart-shape, of wrought iron; Small Circular, or wrought iron, with bossed rim. **Bottom:** Spade, with classic molding, chrysanthemum and crescent, and loop handle; Rocaille Spade shape, with thumb hold. Displays classic Muse of Music and bears legend "Jenny Lind"; Late Spade with "church-window" decoration and Eastlake handle. Bottom row are all of cast iron.

Above, top row: Circular, wrought iron, high footed; Spade, wrought iron, with five cut-out hearts and stamped in legend "FORGET ME NOT"; Ovoid, with points and scrolls. **Center row:** Spade, with simple loops, bearing legend of Patent, and the "patent" a waxing roller just above the openwork handle; Geometric, six circles looped to form stars, and loop handle. **Bottom row:** Circular, wrought iron, with flat button feet; Triangular, with scrolls, and pan handle, wrought iron; Horseshoe, cast iron, openwork date is 1894.

lowing to offer as a contribution toward a classification of patterns. Certainly this task is not exactly a picnic. But we do have the inspiration of Mrs. Ruth Webb Lee who, with courage worthy of an army general, understood . . . and accomplished . . . the Herculean task of classifying all patterns of pressed glassware.

The first attempt at classification should, it would seem, separate these trivets into basic shapes. This, then, is an attempt at such general classification:

Disc, or Circular: Trivets of round shape. Known with and without handles, some very plain and simple and others highly ornate, resembling the so-called Pennsylvania barn symbols, butter molds, et cetera. The vast majority of these very ornate circulars seem to have been cast in New York state foundries, from designs found on carved woodenwares of the Netherlands.

Geometrical: Under this broad category would fall combinations of circles, triangles, squares, and allied forms regardless of the pattern achieved. Known with and without handles.

Heart: A variant of the spade shape, but showing a clearly outlined heart form, known with and without handles.

Horseshoe: One of the favorites with foundries of the latter half of the 19th century. Rarely without handles, frequently with advertisement of maker, but known in a wide variety of decorative styles, all within the horseshoe shape.

Ovoid: Oval shapes with either rounded or pointed ends, with or without handles.

Spade: This shape is obviously designed for use as a flatiron rest. The body of the trivet is spade-shaped, and generally has a handle at the blunt end of the spade. Many spades had cameo portraits of famous people in low relief.

Gridiron: Many varieties, some looking like waffle irons and others like standard gridirons. Known with and without handles.

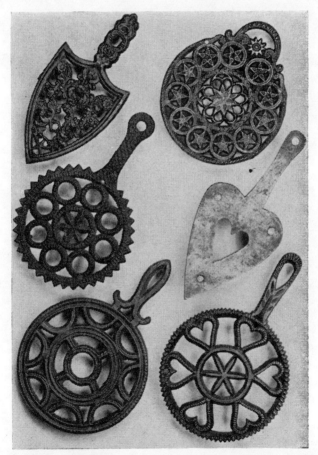

Above, top row: Spade trivet, with armorial scrolls and rococo handle; Circular, with thirteen stars in smaller circles and ten-pointed star at base of stub handle, marked "E. R. Manley". **Center:** Circular, Dutch star and eight circles, saw edge, pan handle; Wrought iron heart with heart cutout and long, or "pan" handle. **Bottom:** Circular, with simple geometric openwork and scroll handle; Circular, six hearts and star with serrated edge and pan-handle. All cast iron except where specifically designated as wrought.

Square: Solid or openwork, with or without surface ornamentation, some with handles but generally without handles.

Star: A rare form. Made with and without handles. 3, 4, 5, 6 and 7-pointed star examples are known.

Triangle: Not a variant of the spade shape, because handled examples are known with handle affixed to a side and others with handle affixed to one of the points. Those with handles are generally in the form of an equilateral triangle.

With this simple recitation of basic forms comes a descriptive problem comparable only to the task that faced Mrs. Lee. Rather than attempt formalized recitation here—for my task is not yet one quarter done and these presented constitute the very first publicity yet released—I will attempt secondary classification as captions under each of the illustration groups.

Toy Trivets to Treasure

by MARGARET H. KOEHLER

THROUGHOUT HISTORY, children have learned by using their own tiny replicas of adult's things. Originally trivets were used to hold cooking pots over an open fire, and later as a resting place while these pots cooled. In more recent times, trivets—in this instance sadiron holders—were made to hold heavy flatirons, and a century or so ago little girls learned how to iron by working on their doll's clothes with miniature versions of their mother's irons and holders.

Some years ago, Mrs. Madeline Thompson started collecting old trivets. One day she found a toy trivet just 3 inches long at an antiques shop. She purchased it for her collection and, as so often happens, one tiny trivet led to another. Before long, she had accumulated several miniatures of their larger counterparts. Mrs. Thompson discovered that toy trivets ranged in size from as little as 2¼ inches long to as much as 5 inches long, and came in a wide variety of shapes and designs. The miniature flatirons too, were just as varied in size and shape. Most toy trivets were made of cast iron, but a few brass ones have been found, also.

Apparently some of the larger miniature trivets were not designed initially as playthings for children; possibly they were salesmen's samples. These were sometimes listed in old catalogs as "half-size" trivets and are fairly easy to detect since they are too large for a toy iron, and too small for a full-size iron.

Collecting toy trivets can inevitably lead to the collecting of other iron toys. One of Mrs. Thompson's favorite iron toys is a tiny coal stove, complete with an array of miniature pots and pans. It occupies a prominent place in her kitchen and seems to compliment her collection of toy trivets.

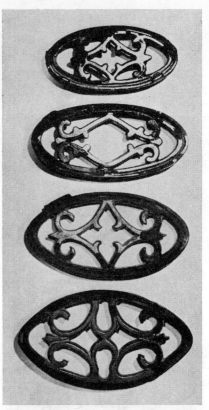

Oval-shaped toy trivets range in size from 3 inches long (top) to nearly 4 inches long (bottom); those shown above are made of cast iron.

This sturdy little sadiron, just 3 inches long, rests on a trivet 5 ½ inches in length.

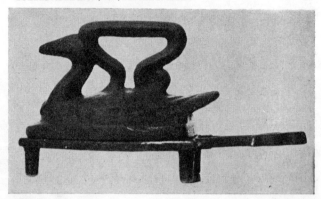

A rare duck-shaped sadiron, 2 ½ inches long, rests on a "Cathedral No. 4" trivet, 3 ½ inches long. In 1865, these were offered "Painted in four colors."

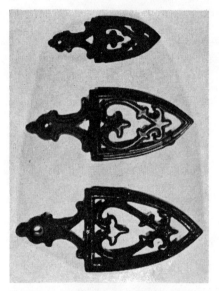

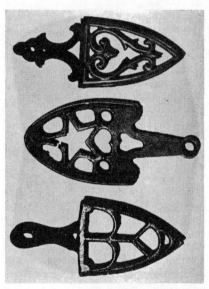

Cast iron toy trivets in the "Cathedral No. 3" pattern can be found in lengths of 2 ¼ inches (top), one of the smallest, to 3 ⅝ inches (bottom).

Some "not quite miniature" trivets measure from 5 inches long (top) to nearly 6 inches long (center); the "Cathedral No. 5" trivet (bottom) is 5 ½ inches long.

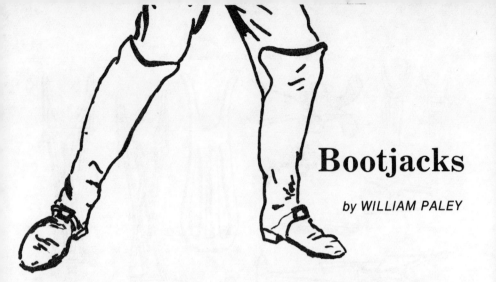

Bootjacks

by WILLIAM PALEY

A BOOTJACK, like a footscraper, usually had its place near the service door of the house—often doing double duty as a doorstop. Its primary function was to assist in removing the high, tight boots, which were fashionable in the eighteenth and nineteenth centuries, without the inconvenience to the wearer of stooping or of soiling his hands. Not only were bootjacks made for gentlemen but for ladies as well, as evidenced by the adjustable and the double-ended types. The Industrial Revolution with its increasing emphasis on travel, and the Civil War which necessitated it, brought about the invention of the small portable and folding bootjacks.

When low-cut, laced shoes became popular late in the nineteenth century, bootjacks, like the boots for which they were designed, became obsolete. Many have survived, however, and some interesting examples can be found in cast and wrought iron, brass, and wood. The several illustrations accompanying this article show a variety of types that can be found.

Illustrations drawn by the author.

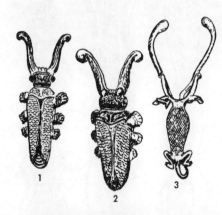

Key to Illustrations

1 and 2: Two versions of the iron beetle bootjack. *3:* Of brass, with two movable mandibles which clamp over the instep of the boot as the heel is forced into place.

4: Variously known as "Naughty Nellie" or "Naughty Lady." *5:* Equipped with a stiff brush and handle for removing caked mud and cleaning boots; this piece is marked "Patd. March 3D 68." *6:* As the prongs retract, the fore-legs fold back against the body making this a very compact portable bootjack.

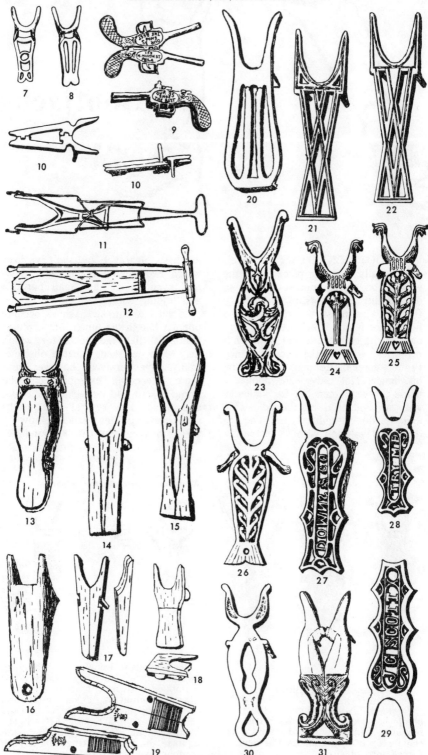

7

8

9

10

10

11

12

13

14

15

16

17

18

19

20

21

22

23

24

25

26

27

28

29

30

31

7: A small, lightweight iron bootjack. 8: One like this is shown in the Bennington Historical Museum; like most iron bootjacks, it is late 19th century. 9: A realistic pistol when closed, and a bootjack when open. 10: Another lightweight folding piece.

11: Of cast iron and wire, this bootjack was designed for someone who could not bend or stoop. The long wire handle can be operated from a standing position, and a wire clamp holds the heel firmly in place while the boot is being removed. 12: The loop in this oak bootjack was designed to hold down the instep of the boot as the foot was withdrawn.

13: An ingenious combination of wood and iron. As pressure is applied by the free foot, the metal prongs close tightly about the heel of the boot. 14 and 15: Neatly made hardwood bootjacks.

16: Bootjack carved from one piece of oak. 17 and 18: Two folding bootjacks made of walnut.

19: The opening for the heel is bound with leather to prevent scuffing the boot; a strip of rubber provides a firm grip for the free foot. 20: A large, heavy cast iron bootjack.

21 and 22: Differ only in the design around the heel opening. 23: A fairly common entwined scroll pattern, cast iron.

24 and 25: Variations on the same design. 26: The fishtail design is somewhat refined in this example.

27, 28 and 29: Cast iron bootjacks marked "Downs & Co.," "Try Me," and "J. G. Scott."

30: Cast iron bootjack with shoe design in center. 31: Two boots form the heel-grip for this cast iron bootjack. The initials "G. R." are impressed on the back. 32: A decorative, but sturdy cast iron bootjack.

33: A rather crudely cast iron bootjack. 34: A simple design in a cast iron bootjack. 35: Cast iron in a plain vertical design.

36: Designed for use as a wrench or a bootjack. 37, 38, 39 and 40: Heavy cast iron bootjacks. 41: Cast iron with a pleasing heart design.

42: Very early cast iron bootjack with heart motifs. 43 and 44: Two different forms with similar designs.

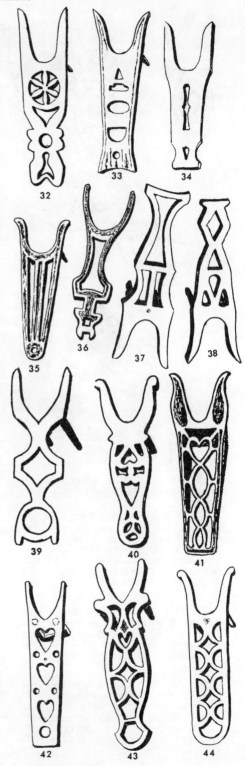

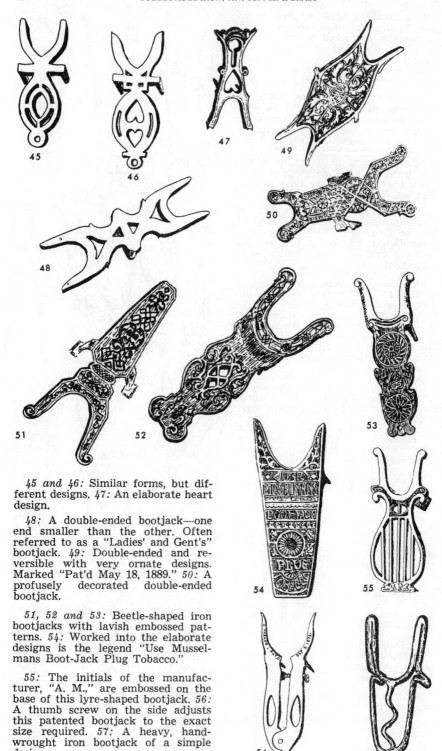

45 and 46: Similar forms, but different designs. *47:* An elaborate heart design.

48: A double-ended bootjack—one end smaller than the other. Often referred to as a "Ladies' and Gent's" bootjack. *49:* Double-ended and reversible with very ornate designs. Marked "Pat'd May 18, 1889." *50:* A profusely decorated double-ended bootjack.

51, 52 and 53: Beetle-shaped iron bootjacks with lavish embossed patterns. *54:* Worked into the elaborate designs is the legend "Use Musselmans Boot-Jack Plug Tobacco."

55: The initials of the manufacturer, "A. M.," are embossed on the base of this lyre-shaped bootjack. *56:* A thumb screw on the side adjusts this patented bootjack to the exact size required. *57:* A heavy, hand-wrought iron bootjack of a simple design.

"Oven" andirons; hollow, with slides for baking potatoes inside

Pre-Stove Cooking

by EDWIN C. WHITTEMORE

BACK THERE in the 1600s and the 1700s, how did your Great-great-great-great-grandmother Hepzibah and your Great-great-great-aunt Piety do the cooking? What were the conditions they had to work under? What were the big differences from today?

First of all, there was no semblance of a constant, steady, even heat. Stoves were not used until the early 1800s, and then only by a few. They were not at all common until the middle of the century. So the source of heat for cooking was the fireplace, roaring hot one minute, ashen and cool a little later. A fundamental problem in cooking was constant re-adjustment to varying cooking temperatures.

Secondly, there may not have been fire there when you wanted it. There were no electric switches, no gas spigots, not even matches. Lighting a

fire with flint and steel by means of the family tinder box was both tricky and tedious, and often took more than a half hour to do. Thérefore, fires were, so far as possible, made perpetual by constant feeding with fuel, skillful banking at night and when not in active use.

Thirdly, there was no refrigeration. The cool depths of the dug well and the corner of the backyard brook helped, but in a limited way.

Fourth, there was no running water. Very occasionally an ingenious home-owner would draw water from a hillside spring to his kitchen by gravity, but this was rare. Water had to be dipped, pumped, lifted and carried—carried in endless repetition.

How in simple terms did those industrious early housewives actually perform the cooking processes, prior to the arrival of the cook stove? There were really two distinct periods, not definable so much by date as describable in terms of the living habits and facilities that created two separate eras. Here are the distinctive marks of the two:

A. The period of: Wooden chimneys, clay lined—Hearths with limited capacity — Wooden lug poles — Dutch Oven baking.

B. The period of: Brick chimneys—Hearths with huge capacity—Iron lug poles—Built-in-chimney baking.

Because of primitive conditions, strictly local sources for the materials, and limited labor supplies, the early years were shy of building materials such as brick. Great wide boards, 30 inches wide and wider, were sawed by hand in the pit, fashioned into chimney form and lined with clay which baked hard, dry, and fire resistant.

Across over head would be a long, freshly cut pole, often of swamp maple which, being green and moist, would last for months before drying out and burning. This lug pole, so-called, was usually about five feet above the floor of the fireplace, the hearth. From it hung all manner of "S" hooks, trammel hooks, either ratchet or tongued, and on them in turn were the various kettles and pots in all manner of shape and size.

On the hearth itself was another series of utensils, all on legs, most with pad feet, ready to be moved forward and back, to and fro, amid the hot coals and the warm ashes to get more or less heat as needed.

Baking in this early period was most often done in a tightly lidded heavy iron pot. Most authorities agree this is the true "Dutch oven," though

the name has often been used for other devices also. This Dutch oven had legs and, most important, a lid so strong and nicely fitted that not only could the oven be set in among the hot coals, but hot coals could also be heaped upon the lid. All kind of baking was done in it.

The second period presents the same theories and practices, but slightly more refined. Brick, made locally or imported as ship's ballast, was used to construct fine big solid fireplaces and chimneys. Iron was being "worked" in the colonies, so the perishable wooden lug poles give way to various types of iron lug poles and back bars, firmly and permanently implanted along the upper reaches of the fireplace.

In place of the Dutch oven, built-in bricked ovens handled the baking. These were large and small; often in a domed beehive shape, at one side, at both sides, or to the rear of the fireplace. They were connected to the chimney with an independent flue.

Of course, neither Dutch ovens nor built-in ovens were always used. It would not be uncommon to push a bed of hot coals and ash to one side of the hearth and bury potatoes directly in it to bake. Andirons were there to hold up the burning logs, and one ingenious person fashioned hollow "box" andirons. The front ends slid forward revealing attached interior trays. Potatoes were put upon them and the trays slid back within the andirons for baking.

Cooking Processes

The actual processes of cooking fell

Top to bottom: large iron skimmer or strainer; pothook with wooden handle; average-size skimmer; wooden toddy ladle.

Small tin reflector oven with spit adjustable to many fixed positions; wire potato boiler or basket.

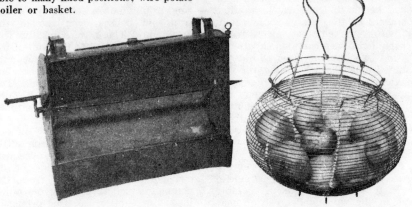

into the same categories as they do. today:

Roasting. In the earliest times the bird or piece of meat was simply suspended from the front edge of the fireplace and made to revolve. Sometimes a child was assigned to this task. Sometimes the busy housewife twisted the suspending cord at handy intervals, letting it "unwind" itself in the opposite direction. Later, revolving spits were used, operated by a descending weight as in a grandfather's clock. There were also mechanical key-wound spring-driven "jacks" for the purpose and, on more occasions that one first realizes, a spit operated by a treadmill on which a dog ran.

Proper capture of the maximum amount of heat and the increased availability of tin produced the reflector oven, or tin kitchen, or hearth kitchen, as it is called. Sitting on short legs, a giant hood with curved back and open front faced the fire. Across it ran a wrought iron spit or skewer which was manually turned a little at a time as necessary. Suitable holes in the tin sidewall, and a properly placed hook or position-setter beside the spit, made many positions possible. To conserve heat there was a hinged "peep hole" in the curved back wall. Through this, the cook could observe how the roast was doing without turning the whole reflector oven. These reflector ovens came in various sizes from about twelve to twenty-four inches.

Baking was chiefly accomplished in the Dutch oven, the built-in-brick chimney oven, and reflector ovens.

Toasting is a form of roasting. There were many toasters. some of them exceptional examples of the fine work that a blacksmith could do in decoration with iron. As a group they were characterized by the various methods of turning or flipping the carrying unit (the toast holder, etc.) so that each side could be exposed to the heat without changing the position of the toaster handle which naturally was kept where it would not get too hot to manipulate.

Broiling, where the meat, fowl, or fish to be cooked was brought close to the heat, is the method where the juices are of great volume, and to the colonists these juices were of great importance. Consequently, every effort was made to catch and save them. A broiler may have been stationary or revolving, and it was often made with grooved arms leading to a reservoir area. The revolving feature, as in the toaster, placed the material near to the flame without having the handle get too close; it also provided an adjustment for greater or less heat, the ever-constant problem with an uneven heat supply.

Boiling and *Stewing* call for the same procedures, but with more or less heat. A variety of pots and kettles were used, often of iron, also of copper and brass. Portable, they could be used anywhere within the fireplace.

It should be pointed out that the huge 8 foot, 10 foot, and larger fireplaces were rarely used for one huge enormous fire. Actually, the sides and corners of the hearth were often used for a bench or small settle so that members of the family could really sit within the chimney for warmth. It would also be a common experience to find two or more fires within the same fireplace at the same time—a medium sized one in the center, perhaps, while a low burning heap of red coals might be performing another cooking process to one side. So there were big pots, little pots, covered pots, open pots, pots with bails, pots with side handles, almost always on legs.

Frying has changed little over the years. In the early days the problem, as in the other methods of cooking, was in the varying degrees of heat available, and in the practical problem of handling the hot pans over an open fire. One s o l u t i o n was the long-handled wrought-iron frying pan, a common item. More rare and more interesting were the revolving frying pans on legs, with a handle. Actually, there were a great many kinds, sizes, and styles of fry pans in the equipment of early kitchens. Interesting note — there were almost never any small ones.

Comes the Crane

The crane which replaced the lug pole, and which became such an important central unit of hearth or fireplace cooking, is said to have been an American invention, but that is questionable. The crane is the horizontal arm suspended from the side wall of the fireplace and swinging out as desired into any one of many positions. It gradually replaced the lug pole, often was supplementary to it.

The manner in which a large heavy duty crane was installed in a fireplace explains why the original suspending rings or pintel units are rarely rescued from old houses even though the cranes are. There were usually five thicknesses of brick to the wall of the fireplace. The pintel pins not only went through these five layers but also had right angle terminals. The stock was heavy iron bar stock. They could not have been removed without tearing down the chimney!

In some homes there was another built-in cooking unit — an iron kettle set into brick, much as the oven was built. With a fire and flue of its own, or taking its heat from the chimney which it abutted, the built-in or "set" kettle was used primarily as a source of hot water, for "scalding" pigs, and for other tasks calling for a large container of hot liquid.

Food and Equipment

There was romance, variety, and ingenuity connected with products accessory to the cooking processes. Salt was done without, was made from sea water, even imported, until sources of salt were developed in this country. Spices were obtainable through import, being compact and of high value, and were used even more than they are today. Sugar was scarce, came in heavy cones and was cut into chunks with special sugar cutters, then pulverized in crushers. Only city folk had it. Those in the country depended on honey, molasses and maple syrup.

There was variety and ingenuity, too, in the tools or equipment of the cooking area, crude as they may have been. There were all sorts of ladles,

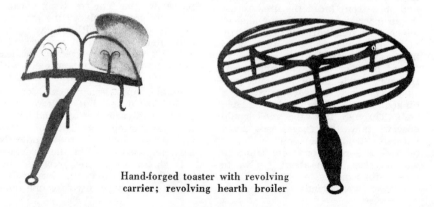

Hand-forged toaster with revolving carrier; revolving hearth broiler

strainers, and dippers; there were herb drying racks and herb grinders. There were sieves with wood frames and lovely plaid-design woven horsehair mesh. There were graters, large and small, simple and complex. There were rotary apple parers and potato parers. There were lard presses, food choppers, countless different sizes and shapes in mortars and pestles. There were large and small pot hooks of iron, or wood and iron, with which hot containers could be handled. Wood and iron were the usual materials but brass and copper were also used.

"Mixture" dishes were the order of the day –– porridges, stews, broths, mush, and hash. A big kettle was kept simmering over the fire almost continuously, and a newly-shot rabbit or squirrel would be dressed and popped into it. Because potatoes disintegrated if cooked too long, they were often placed in a globe-like potato basket of wire, and set down into the simmering kettle, being removed when done, as the whole simmered on. Similar contrivances were used for foods such as eggs. There was considerable of this cooking-within-cooking.

To accompany the meal, the beverage was very often beer or hard cider, both of which were normally preferred to water. The table was extreme simplicity. There were wood and horn spoons, no forks, few knives, much eating from the fingers.

Iron Match Safes

Six of the sixty-six match safes in the Dickinson Collection.

SOMEONE has said that over 500 different categories of interest wait upon the collector who takes the plunge. The more we visit the homes and offices of collectors of the unusual, the more we think the anonymous commentator missed the mark by 500 categories, at least.

Mr. Harry P. Dickinson is a manufacturing jeweler who, perhaps, tiring of gold, silver and platinum, turned to cast iron. He wanted something "little" to collect; again, perhaps something not too far removed from his own association with small but precious items. One day, on Cape Cod, he bought an unique little hinged box on a hanger which they told him was a match safe.

Now he owns between sixty-five and seventy cast iron match safes, all different. The most unusual one is a Church match safe, featuring a Gothic arch, in outline, with a Gargoyle from Notre Dame serving as the container, the cap being hinged and serving as a lid. Another intriguing one is a miniature grinding mortar, issued as an advertisement for the maker of the Grinding Mills, located at Easton, Pennsylvania. There are two and three tiered examples which, Mr. Dickinson says, were made to accommodate both live and burnt matches. Thus far, this collector has not started on mechanical match safes, but there are such items; there are storks, pelicans, monkeys and other beasties who gyrate, peck and pick into a slot and lo, up they come with one match.

Clockwork Roasting Jacks of Iron and Brass

by DAVID CLARKE

CLOCKWORK roasting jacks, those handsome and ingenious little machines whose purpose was to turn the meat roasting before the open fire, were in use in the first half of the 19th century. Apparently most of them were made in Sheffield, England, and from the scarcity of examples to be found in America today compared to the number available in England, it would seem they were in more common use in the mother country.

These efficient kitchen aids hung from a shackle or bracket fastened to the chimneypiece. The roast was hung on the hook below. Sometimes a jack is found to which has been added a small cast iron wheel with several hooks below which could carry a number of steaks or other small items at once.

These little machines were cased in well polished sheet brass and bore the maker's name on a decorative stamped brass label. They were provided with an iron clock key, and the keyhole was given a neat swinging coverplate.

The jack made by Linwood is the type most usually found today. Another variety, made by Chesterman (still a prominent name in Sheffield engineering circles) used a slightly different movement in a case of squatter shape. The Restells Patent Jack, manufactured by E. B. Bennett, was of banjo shape and had a permanently fitted brass winder in the center of the casing.

John Linwood seems to have been the most prolific maker. His clockwork movement seems crude, yet in reality it was a triumph of design over the limitations imposed by the materials and technology of the period. The designers, not having an efficient thrust bearing available to support the load,

Linwood-made jack hangs from a typical brass bracket fixed above the fireplace, and shows wheel attachment from which steaks or small items could be hung.

had to devise a mechanism with the minimum of friction in order to conserve the energy of the spring and so make a long running machine.

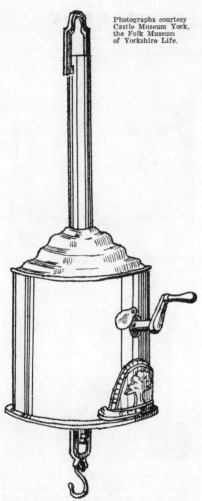

Photographs courtesy
Castle Museum York,
the Folk Museum
of Yorkshire Life.

vertical pin which is the pivot of a quadrant driving through a train of gears to the final hook. It is this hook with its concentric pinion that is suspended by the silk.

A refinement usually included was a spring loaded clutch at the hook to prevent it from turning when the jack was not in use.

The jack was made to work for long periods under difficult conditions without attention. Today they are eagerly sought by connoisseurs of clockwork as well as collectors of culinary equipment.

Most usual type of clockwork roasting jack found today. Author's collection.

This was done by carrying the load on a skein of silk thread anchored at the top of the tubular extension. This could not, of course, twist more than a few times before offering resistance and the rotation was therefore reversed after every two or three revolutions. There was an added advantage in that a governor was not required to control the speed, the meat just revolved gently to and fro.

This movement has an anchor type escapement reminiscent of that in a long case clock. The spring drives the escapement wheel through a pair of gears. The teeth on this wheel impinge alternately on projections from a

This jack works above a "hastener", or sheet iron Dutch oven, which was placed in front of the fire.

Household Ironwares

by DORIS S. WOOLF

MOST collectors of early Americana respond to the homely appeal of household items in wrought and cast iron. From visits to museums, historic houses and antiques shops, we are familiar with the intriguing list of collectible ironware —the firebacks and stove plates; fanciful toasters and grills; long-handled skillets and slices with their charming terminals; toddy sticks and tongs; skimmers, ladles, and spoons; quaintly shaped teakettles, Betty lamps, and the relatively rare lacy-handled posnets. Although these numerous hearth and culinary items that have come down to us have, for the most part, lost their purely utilitarian value, they are rich in historical significance and useful decorative accessories in creating early-day atmosphere in the increasingly popular Early American home.

1. *Top shelf: Rush light, mortar and pestle, lamb door stop, "bee hive" string holder, charcoal stove iron. Middle shelf: Lacy-handled cast-iron posnets. Bottom shelf: 18th century handled pot for open hearth cooking, covered Dutch oven, wood-burning stove kettle.*

History proves that iron was the first native metal utilized by the colonists. In 1630 a rich deposit of bog-iron was found at Saugus, Massachusetts, near Boston. A company was founded and a hammer, smelter and a foundry were set up for producing both wrought and cast iron. Thus was born one of the earliest New England industries. The

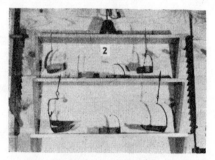

2. *Collection of ratchet lights and Betty lamps; rush light on top shelf.*

3. *Long-handled skillet, Pennsylvania heart-shaped waffle iron, three-legged skillet, peel or slice, saw-toothed trammel.*

enterprise flourished and supplied our first colonists with the necessary pots, kettles, hinges, locks and latches and the impressive battery of fireplace equipment that was seen on every hearth at this time, when all cooking and heating came from the log fire on the open hearth.

During the first years of American colonization, fat-burning Betty lamps, not much changed in form from the ancient Roman lamps, were used; later, when candles were dipped at home, the smith's business grew even more brisk in the making of iron candlesticks. The original Saugus foundry expanded and established other forges in 1648 and 1652 at Braintree and Raynham, Massachusetts. With expanding colonization and the new forges, the production of our collector's items grew enormously—to such an extent that there are enough of these simple, delightfully wrought iron pieces for every one of us to possess at least a few of them. And to own an item of 17th or 18th century American iron is to provoke an interest in the history and origin of man's use of this least expensive and most adaptable of all metals.

From the standpoint of style and design, the best American iron was made from the time of the Revolution to the end of the 18th century. After 1800 there was a rapid decline in the production of American hand wrought ironwork, except in Pennsylvania where the ancient traditions of the blacksmiths continued to flourish and the production of excellent ironware continued as late as the mid-19th century. Because of the persistence of Pennsylvania smiths to continue the old methods and the lingering traditions in other Eastern states, despite the advancement of the Machine Age, collectors of today enjoy abundant examples of early American ironware.

5. *Hearth display: round revolving grill, toggle-arm pipe tongs, Betty lamp, double Phoebe lamp, spatula, spoons, peel, fork, "spider", trivet, and kettle.*

4. *Collection of grills, toasters, wrought iron handled bed warming pan, short trammel.*

Wall Lavabo of agate-enameled stamped sheet iron, made by the Central Stamping Company of Saint Louis, Missouri, 1889, for the Western Cottage trade.

Wafer Irons *by MARY EARLE GOULD*

A wafer was a form of unleavened bread used in religious ceremonies. As early as 1358, a wafer iron used in making wafers was mentioned in an appraisement of goods belonging to an English gentleman:—"one pair of irons for the Eucharist." The wafers were used with wine at the sacrament of the Lord's Supper.

A wafer iron (or tongs) is a utensil with two hinged parts, fashioned of iron by the blacksmith. It has two round plates or heads, measuring about six inches in diameter and the handles are three feet long, such as were on all implements used in the fireplace. Some early irons bear a seal with three locked hearts surmounted by a cross enclosed within a circle, and an anchor with ornaments imitating leaves. Some have a crucifix or a sacred monogram. All of the irons show that they were used exclusively in ceremonial services.

Among the bride's gifts was a wafer iron, with the date of the marriage and the initials of the giver, usually the groom. This gift was an omen of good luck. One such wafer iron in the author's collection, is (illus.), marked 1785 with the initials W C M. There is a heart and scroll on one head and on the other two hex marks and a simple scroll. These incisions were not cut in the reverse, so the dates and initials on the wafer iron were not as they should be on the wafer. The art of reversed stamping was doubtless of little concern in those early years.

The wafers or wafer cakes were made by a waferer and two or three irons were sufficient in supplying a community for any ceremony. It must have been a tedious task for one man to manage the irons and make a great number of cakes. The iron was first heated over a charcoal fire or in the embers of a fireplace, before the batter was put into the heads. There are rests in some collections of early implements on which any long-handled iron could be held while cooking over the fire. These rests are frames with three or four legs from which extend an arm on which the handle of the iron rested. The wafer iron or the

waffle iron was extremely heavy and these rests relieved the worker from holding the implement over the hot embers. A dealer in the cakes was called a wafer, or it was a wafer woman who sold the cakes.

As the years went on, the types of wafer irons changed and various shaped heads appeared, being oval as well as round. A short-handled wafer iron shows that the wafers continued to be made when stoves replaced open fireplaces. There is a projection on this type of iron which rested on the rim of the stove hole, and the handles are short. (see illus.)

In this country the wafers were used in the home as well as in the church. The irons were made by local blacksmiths and the patterns on the

(Left) Early wafer iron dated 1785, initials WCM, two hex marks and heart. (Right) Later wafer iron with short handles and a protruding nub which rested in stove hole.

heads were flowers, initials and dates, and the necessary hex mark. This hex mark was supposed to keep away evil spirits, (witches in particular) and was used on doors, tools and utensils, expressing the confidence of the owner for his protection against evil spirits.

A rule for making wafers or wafer cakes is given in a cook book called Two Fifteenth-Century C o o k e r y Books. "Waffres — Take the womb (belly) of a luce (full-grown pike) and sethe here wyl and do it on a mortar and tender cheese thereto, grynde them togethir; then take flour and white of Eyren (obsolete word for eggs) and beat them togethir and look that the cyrcun (iron) be hot and lay thereon a thin paste and then make waffyrs and so on."

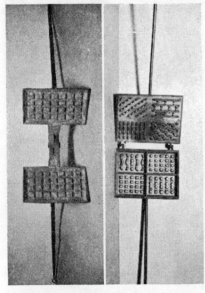

Early waffle irons. The one on the right has different patterns in each section.

From a cook book of the early 19th century, it would seem that wafers continued to be used. By then their use was for home as well as for church ceremonies. A rule reads:— "Dry the flour well which you intend to use, mix a little pounded sugar and finely pounded mace with it; then make it into a thick batter with cream; butter the wafer irons, let them be hot; put a teaspoonful of batter into them, so bake them carefully, and roll them off the iron with a stick." Sometimes the rolled wafers were filled with whipped cream and sealed at the ends with a preserved strawberry.

Waffles and waffle irons are more commonly known today than wafers and wafer irons. In the early centuries, there was a Waffling Sunday in Sweden similar to the Wafering Sunday of old England. On that particular Sunday, the people of the communities went from one home to another and were served waffles. It was a social gathering of the communities connected with their religion.

A rule for waffles used more than one hundred years ago reads: — One quart flour and a teaspoon salt. One quart sour milk with two teaspoonsful melted butter in it. Five well-beaten eggs. A teaspoon or more of salaratus, enough to sweeten the milk. Bake in waffle iron. Waffle irons well oiled with lard each time they are used.

The old waffle irons have oblong heads, with a block pattern. The irons were hand wrought by the blacksmiths. When the manufacturing of iron tools came about, the shape of the waffle iron became more fancy and these were stamped with a date or with a number. Many irons are in the shape of a heart. One of the illustrations is an early hand wrought iron with both heads alike, while another illustration has eight section with a different pattern in each section.

Such records of the early years bring to us of the 20th century a history of that first Mother's Sunday. Three hundred years ago, the observance was established. Love, honor and respect brought about the day and in our modern custom, there should be that same love, honor and respect.

Iron Apple Parers

by ALAN ANDERSON & WILLIAM THOMAS

Fig. 1: Unmarked wooden parer, only slightly different from the model patented by Reuben and Amos Mosher, in 1829. On display at Huntington (N.Y.) Historical Society.

APPLES WERE a staple commodity in early 19th century New England and other settled localities in America. They were pressed into cider, dried, strung, made into apple butter and apple sauce. They were fried, stewed, baked, cooked into pies and other pastries, like dumplings and Brown Bettys. Since so many of these edibles required that the apple be peeled, ingenious Yankees were quick to invent and put into use mechanical apple parers.

The earliest American parer now known is a wooden one designed and

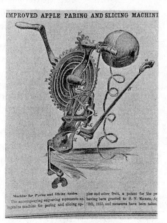

Fig. 2: Improved Apple Paring and Slicing Machine, 1856.

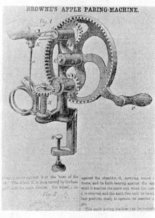

Fig. 3: Browne's Apple Paring Machine, 1855.

Fig. 4: Alcott's Apple Corer, 1859.

Fig. 5: Manufactured by Goodell Co., Antrim, N.H.; patented March 18, 1884.

built around 1750. Until about 1849, when cast metal parers appeared, apple parers were made of wood, except for the metal knives.

The first recorded U.S. patent for a parer was granted to Moses Coates, Downing Fields, Pa., in February 1803. In the next 35 years, several other patents for wooden parers were issued. They went to S. Crittenden, Connecticut, Aug. 1809; Willard Badger, Massachusetts, Feb. 16, 1809; Cyrus Gates, Rutland, Vt., Dec. 15, 1810; Reuben and Amos Mosher, Saratoga County, N.Y., Dec. 28, 1829; A. Glendenning, Loudon County, Va., Sept. 9, 1823; Cyprian C. Pratt, Paris, Me., Dec. 28, 1833; Daniel Davis II, Tolland County, Conn., March 14, 1834; Robert W. Mitchell, Martins Hill, Ohio, April 13, 1838; and J. W. Hatcher, Bedford County, Va., Feb. 3, 1836.

Most of these parers operated on the same principle, but all had variations acceptable for patent rulings. Skilled home craftsmen, copying patented models on their own lathes, produced many personal variations. Yet the parers all achieved the same end. The apple was impaled on a fork and by simple or complicated means, was skinned by the rotation of the parer with a knife blade held against it.

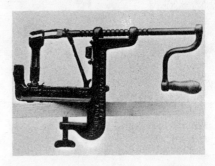

Fig. 7: Manufactured by Goodell Co., Antrim, N.H.; no patent date appears on it.

Fig. 8: Unmarked; possibly a copy of one of the Goodell patents.

Fig. 6: Also manufactured by Goodell Co., patented March 24, 1898, marked "White Mountain APE"; designated as the "Turntable '98" model.

Fig. 9: No manufacturer's name on this, but the patent dates of May 5, 1858, June 7, 1870, and March 26, 1872, appear.

Fig. 10: Patented by H. Keyes, June 17 and Dec. 16, 1856.

Fig. 11: No markings; possibly a metal variation of Julius Weed's wooden parer and slicer.

Fig. 12: Known as the Turntable Apple Parer, this bears the same patent dates, June 17 and Dec. 16, 1856, as the Keyes model, but also carries the name of Lockley and Howland.

Some parers operated by direct drive; some by belt drive; others had a coupling of a large wooden wheel with ratchets engaging a small wheel carrying the apple fork; still others employed multiple gears to speed up the apple and the paring operation.

The *Scientific American* for December 1, 1849, carried an illustrated account of what appears to be the first patented metal parer. Juliu(s) Weed of Painesville, Ohio, was the holder of the patent, dated July 31, 1849. (Fig. 13) Though partially constructed of wood, the principal mechanisms were of metal. Its special feature was that it not only pared, but also cored and sliced the apple.

In the August 11, 1855 issue, *Scientific American* showed Browne's Apple Paring Machine. (Fig. 3), invented by J. D. Browne of Cincinnati, Ohio, who called it "a very compact and simple machine for paring apples and other fruit."

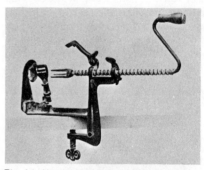

Fig. 14: No markings; possibly a variation of the Goodell Co. parer.

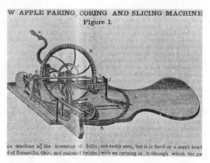

Fig. 13: Julius Weed's invention, patented July 31, 1849.

Alcott's Apple Corer (Fig. 4) was shown in the April 2, 1859 issue of *Scientific American*. The article accompanying the diagram stated, in part: "This machine may also be made into a parer by placing the three pronged holder, J, over I, and placing the apple upon it, it can be pared very quickly by hand."

The only other parer illustrated in *Scientific American* appeared March 22, 1856, and was listed as the Improved Apple Paring and Slicing Machine. (Fig. 2) The accompanying

Fig. 15: Manufactured by C. E. Hudson, Leominster, Mass.; patented Jan. 24, 1889.

Fig. 16: "Made only by the Reading Hardware Co., Reading, Pa.; patents dated May 5, 1868, May 3, 1875, Oct. 19, 1875, Nov. 14, 1875, May 22, 1877.

description shows clearly the operation of this model and all others similar to it:

"The machine is small nearly all its parts being of cast-iron the whole weighing only 2 lb. 10 oz. The contrivance is secured to the table by means of the clamp, A, and to this is attached the standard, B, by means of the strong joint at B, which permits the careening of the machine both right and left. E is the driving wheel, motion being given by means of the crank to all the parts. Upon the face of the driving wheel E, is an inclined scroll, R, upon which one end of the rack bar, G, glides; this rack connects with, and gives motion to, the loop gear H, which supports and guides the spring rod, I, upon which is affixed the paring knife, J.

"The machine being careened, as shown in the cut, an apple is placed upon the fork, K, when by rotation of

Fig. 17: Patented Oct. 6, 1863; no other markings.

Fig. 18: Similar to the Goodell parers, but unmarked.

the crank the driving wheel, E, gives motion to the pinion, E, and thence to the fork and apple, while the scroll, F, acting through the rack bar, G, upon the loop gear, H, the paring knife, J, is thereby passed, during the rotation of the apple, from its base around to its outer end, and effectively pares the apple, when the outer circuit of the scroll, F, having passed the end of the rack bar, G, the coiled spring attached to the other and lower end of the rack bar, contracts, and returns the rack bar, loop gear, spring rod, and paring knife to their original positions in readiness to repeat the operation of paring.

"Without removing the apple from the fork the machine is now careened in an opposite direction, when the pin, L, which secures the loop gear, H, within its socket, comes in contact with the tripping post, M, causing the partial revolution of the loop gear, and thereby withdrawing the end of the rack bar, G, from the scroll, F, thus permitting the backward rotation of

the crank and driving wheel, together with the fork and apple. The slicing arm, N, which is the one hinged to the standard, B, and sustains the slicing knife, O, is now swung by the left hand and pressed lightly against the apple, which is thereby cut into one continuous slice or ribbon, leaving only the core, in cylindrical form upon the fork.

"The careening of the machine perfectly accomplishes the separation of the slices from the parings, while the parabolic curvature of the slicing knife produces such a formation of slices that they do not pack closely together while drying and yet are not in the least objectionable for immediate cooking. This is a novel contrivance; that it works well we know from actual experiment. More information may be obtained, by letter, of the proprietors, Maxam and Smith, Shelburne Falls, Mass."

The rest of the parers illustrated are from the collection of Elsa Anderson of Huntington, N.Y. They give a fine display of the varieties of metal parers available. Only the advent of cast iron made this variety and large production possible. Notice in this assemblage of parers the useless complexity of some, and the utter simplicity of others. All had one single purpose, the paring of apples as quickly as possible.

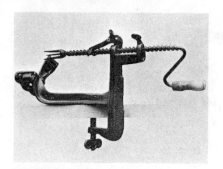

Fig. 19: Similar to the Goodell parers, but unmarked.

Unless otherwise noted, all photographed apple parers are from the collection of Elsa Anderson, Huntington, N.Y. Photos by Alan Anderson.

Early Iron Lighting Devices

by EDWIN C. WHITTEMORE

IN THE earlier types of lighting devices, it is noticeable that a high percentage are of a sort where the position of the light can be raised and lowered in relation to the person using it.

Lighting collectors are often crudely awakened, and even disappointed, the first time they actually test an early lighting device. Observed in a dark room, the light is amazingly insignificant; it can be compared to that of a wooden kitchen match or a small candle. This slight amount of illumination given off by rush lights, Betty lamps, grease lamps, etc., probably explains the great attention given to the adjustability of the light to a desired level. The user wanted it placed where it would do him the most good!

What to Look For

An interesting approach to the study of early lighting is to examine the many types in terms of classifying them according to the methods of this up-and-down adjustment. There are eight easily recognizable types, and a lighting collection that included at least one of each would be outstanding.

In simple terms, these are the eight classifications:

1. Dependence on what the lighting fixture rests upon. *Example:* a tin Ipswich Betty Lamp with its weighted cone base.

2. Dependence upon the point from which the fixture is suspended. *Example:* wrought iron loom light with vertical bar to hang down from nail or peg at variable heights.

3. Dependence on varying the height of the suspending unit. *Example:* the trammel-type fixture with paired members that can shorten or lengthen the vertical height.

4. Dependence on spiral-cut or screw-type central unit around which the candle or lamp carrier rests. *Example:* the sought-after revolving candlestand with crossbar.

5. Dependence on friction wedging. *Example:* a candle-carrying crossbar held to any position on a vertical shaft by a wedge.

6. Dependence on the spring tension of metals. *Example:* a hog-scraper iron candlestick. The movable platform holding up the candle stays where it is put by tension between it and the wall of the tube.

7. Dependence on spaced notches or holes in the vertical member. *Example:* a slot-type vertical candlestand.

8. Dependence on turnscrew wedging. *Example:* a crossbar candlestand where the bar rests on a separate turnscrew, fitting into the vertical member.

Left to right: iron hog-scraper candlestick (#6); table or miniature revolving candlestand (#4); wood-based candlestand of the 17th century with spiral-cut iron top section (also #4).

The Conestoga wagon at the Pennsylvania Farm Museum at Landis Valley was made in 1812. Still in possession of its original parts, it clearly shows the skill of the blacksmith who "ironed" it.

Conestoga Ironwork

by PHYLLIS T. BALLINGER

IN THE days when our nation was young, and a principal source of food for its exploding population came from the rich farm lands of Lancaster County in southeastern Pennsylvania, Conestoga wagons carried tons of produce to the bustling cities and returned with dry goods to be used in rural areas. The wagoner was the only person to direct these vehicles, and the responsibility for its maintenance was entirely his own.

The wagon was equipped with all that was required to keep the vehicle operative. A tool box, always painted blue, the traditional color of the wagon bed, was attached to the left side of the wagon. Its hinges and hasp were often ornate, usually symmetri-cal, and always firmly riveted for extra strength. The decorative ironwork on the tool box is considered the height of the blacksmith's craft, for it is here that one finds the most handsomely wrought of all the "ironing" on the wagon. The padlock was of like quality, sturdy but artfully made. The feed box, which hung on the rear of the wagon, was another item which was reinforced with decorative ironwork.

Approximately 15 x 20 x 7 inches, the tool box contained such things as an extra doubletree pin, utility hammer, pincers, nuts and bolts, snap rings, "S" links for repairing chains, bridle bits, and horseshoeing equipment. If a repair had to be made along the way, the wagoner built a fire by the roadside, used the tire of the wagon for an anvil and became his own blacksmith. Although he developed considerable skill in working with iron, the wagoner's work is clearly discernible from that of the professional blacksmith. This can be seen in examining chains used on the wagon. Some, made in very intricate linking patterns, have an obviously replaced link interrupting momentarily the beautiful design of the original.

While these artful chains, fashioned by the blacksmith, greatly appeal to collectors, the somewhat clumsily repaired links also appeal to those who are captivated by the romance of the period. They call to mind the trials and tribulations of the wagoners, and the great contribution made by these men to our country's growth and well-being.

Among other ironwork found on Conestoga wagons which are eagerly

Wagon jacks, made by the blacksmith who did the "ironing" on the Conestoga wagon, are among the few dated tools to be found.

Interesting ironwork can be found on Conestoga wagon tool boxes.

Drawings of various decorated axe rests. Affixed to the hound tree of the Conestoga wagon, they combined utility with artistry.

collected today are the axe rest, the collar placed on the tongue of the wagon (frequently called the "hound band"), the ornamental piece that was placed on the end of the tongue for a practical purpose, and the stay chain hooks.

The axe rest was an object upon which the blacksmith could again display his skill in making decorative ironwork. Floral patterns, geometric designs, or little scrolls can sometimes be found on this piece of equipment —the writer has seen one in the shape of a nicely proportioned fish.

The hound band often had initials cut into it, and the year the wagon was built. On some, the date was stamped into the metal with a star punch, adding a flourish to the overall design. At times the date was outlined with intricate border designs.

The strips of iron, the rear hound plates, the coupling pole pins, and the stay chain hooks were sometimes wrought with artistic touches, too. On these, hearts and tulips, snake heads or the entire body of a coiled snake are to be found over and over in slightly different forms.

No discussion of the ironwork found on the Conestoga wagon would be complete without mentioning the wagon jack. This was used to raise the wheel high enough to clear the ground when repairs were necessary; it was also used to free a wheel from a rut in the road. Approximately 24 x 7 x 3 inches in size, it was standard equipment for the wagon and when not in use it hung on the rear axletree. Made on the principal of modern jacks with rachet type expansion, it cradled the spoke or axle and lifted a considerable weight when the handle was turned. Two spurs on the base of the jack precluded any chance of its slipping while in use.

Straight and curved chisels in various sizes and a circular punch were used to hammer in the initials and numbers found on hound bands and wagon jacks. These simple tools, which the blacksmith made himself, produced quaint effects that collectors find desirable.

In the writer's collection is a wagon jack dated 1859 which was found at Intercourse, Pa. Having survived the Conestoga wagon for which it was originally made, it was used to repair farm wagons for generations. This jack has an interesting though not uncommon feature in connection with the date. The numeral "1" is made with two "Js," the second reversed and with a line joining them to form the letter "H." It has been suggested by Henry K. Landis who, with his brother George, founded what has become the Pennsylvania Farm Museum at Landis Valley, Lancaster County, Pa., that this symbol represented *Jahr Herr Jesu*,—"in the year of our Lord."

The same marking can be found on old chests, date stones, and cast iron stove lids.

Our jack now leans against the fireplace in the den where it recalls legends of a colorful era in American history. After removing the rust and dirt which had accumulated over a period of years, we gave the jack a protective coat of wax. One antiques dealer suggested that we spruce up the old iron by removing the rust with steel wool, cover it with old fashioned black stove polish, and then buffing it to a dull luster.

Western movies, TV shows, and novels have made us conscious of the Conestoga wagon and the part it played in the development of our nation. For about 100 years, from 1740 to 1840, these "ships of inland commerce" were seen in great numbers. One contemporary writer, Morris Birbeck, said, in 1817, "About 12,000 wagons passed between Baltimore and Philadelphia and this place [Pittsburgh] in the last year." By 1840, however, railroads and canals had taken over the freight traffic, and the Conestoga wagons were slowly pushed into oblivion. The accoutrements of the wagon, its fancy ironwork, and the charming little hames bells, which have a story of their own to tell, have now become collector's items.

Illustrations courtesy of the Pennsylvania Historical & Museum Commission, Harrisburg, Pa.

Portable Early Iron Footscraper

AS A RULE, early iron footscrapers were firmly embedded in the brick or stonework of steps or stoop. They were adjuncts of the house and belonged to it forever. This one, of hand-wrought iron, from the collection of Mr. Ray O. Hill, Beaver Falls, Pennsylvania, is portable, mounted on a solid, very heavy block of wood. It could be carried from door to door, wherever it was most needed, or from house to house. Apparently it was set this way originally, a makeshift to suit someone's particular needs.

Such a mounting is well adapted for use today when household moves are many and frequent, and a collector who treasures an early footscraper may want to use it, but hesitates to affix it permanently.

A Sampling of Sad Irons

by A. H. GLISSMAN

THE TERM "sad iron" is of ancient descent. The words "sad" and "sorrowful" existed together in English usage in the 14th century, and we find Chaucer using the word "sorrowful" in its present day meaning. "Sad," however, could mean "solid, dense, compact, or heavy," a meaning now obsolete. "Two grete ymages of golde sad," was written in the 14th century, and another early chronicle, ca. 1330, refers to "with iron nayles sad, his fete was schod."

About 1388, Wyclif in translating the Bible from Latin to English, gave Exodus 38-7 as "Forsoth thilke auter was not sad but holowe."

The word usage wore well; more than two hundred and fifty years later, in 1641, a book on farming advised, "Short barley strawe is the best for stoppinge of holes, because it is sadder and not soe subject to blowe out with everie Blast of winds, as other light and dry strawe is."

As for "sad iron," the earliest printed English reference appears to be in Babbage's *On Economy of Machines and Manufactures,* published in 1832, in which he refers to "sad irons and other castings." The following year, in 1833, J. Holland, in *Manufacturing Metal,* wrote, "Dealers commonly distinguish these useful implements by the terms: sad-iron, box-iron, and Italian iron," indicating that

the term was by no means a recent one.

Appreciation is expressed to Mr. R. K. Blumenau, History Division, Malvern College, Worcester, England, for historical background on the term "sad iron." Additional comments may be found in the *Oxford University Dictionary*, edited by Sir James Murray, 1914 edition.

MEXICO

1. The large handles of these "tattle-tale bell" irons are hollow and contain a ball which rings when the iron is moved. The story goes this was to tell when the maid was shirking; actually, when the handle is gripped, the bell can no longer be heard. All are handmade, and each is different.

2. 19th century, handmade. Many flowered irons come from Mexico. Though they resemble love token irons, the Spanish or Mexican groom never gave his bride something to work with as a wedding present; friends might do so, and he might later on.

ENGLAND

3. 19th century English irons had a sad base but hollow handle.

4. Charcoal burner, mid-19th century. Brass heat shield is decorated with British seal showing lion, unicorn, and crown, and the name "Victoria."

FRANCE

5. Late 19th century commercial launderer, used on a cast iron stand with a small ironing board mounted on it. A bar with a spring tension hooked in the hole in front of the handle to add pressure.

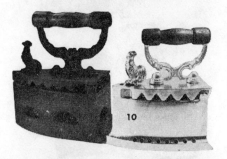

ALSACE-LORRAINE

6. Box iron, 17th century, possibly earlier. Small pieces of leather remaining on the original wool cover of the handle indicate it was once leather covered. This style of long pointed iron is typical of the Alsace-Lorraine section, famous in early days for its ironworks, also of Switzerland. It was heated by an iron slug, warmed in the hearth. Usually a couple of extra "heaters" were kept in the fire.

SWITZERLAND

7. Early 19th century, with shield and white cross of the country as decoration; asbestos heat shield was added later.

HOLLAND

8. Thin brass charcoal burner of the type used in Holland since the 18th century. Sad irons and charcoal burners of the heavier cast iron were introduced in the latter half of the 19th century.

GERMANY

9. Box iron, 18th century; brass shell, iron handle; iron slug, partially shown, was heated in the hearth and inserted in iron.

10. *Left,* charcoal iron, ca. 1800; still being made, but with "K" on the handle instead of "G". *Right,* Japanese reproduction, with thin coating of highly polished brass.

AUSTRIA

11. Alcohol burning travel set, ca. 1860-1900; many were sold in the U.S. around 1900. Trivet (upper right, in case) is for the tank and burner, which can be removed by lifting out if iron gets too hot.

RUSSIA

12. Made in Lindengraph, ca. 1790-1800, this iron has two heaters. In later years, the pin was hinged and was part of the cover; handles were also made in decorative styles.

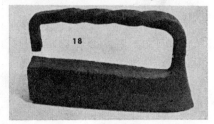

CHINA

13. Charcoal irons were known in China before the time of Christ. This one is very old, though the inscription on the side, referring to one of the four lakes of China and a wall built by Tu Wing Loy, has not yet been satisfactorily translated. Handle is not original, but was carved from horn and installed later.

14. Beautiful replacements of ancient Chinese irons, strictly for tourist trade; they are soldered and would fall apart if heated; some are very old, some are new.

15. Japanese reproduction of a Chinese iron, very large; handle holder is roughly brazed on; handle tilts too high for comfort or use.

CEYLON

16. Charcoal or wood burner, 11" long; weighs 13 lbs.; handmade of heavy brass. This type was used for hundreds of years in parts of Europe and Asia, and is still being used.

KOREA

17. Charcoal iron, brass with teakwood handle. In the Orient, the kimonas were separated by pulling a string so they could be ironed flat with pan-shaped irons. They were then put back together and the wrinkle made in assembling was touched up with the tiny iron, which was heated over the charcoal in the pan.

UNITED STATES

18. Tailor's goose, 18th century, handmade from one piece of iron. Open end of handle allowed it to be hung on a rod over an open fire with the ironing surface next to the hot coals.

19. Polishing iron, made by M. A. N. Cook Company; first patented in 1848.

20. Charcoal iron by Cummings, Taliaferro and Bless, patented 1852; also made under the names "Cummings and Bless," and "Bless and Drake." Bless was known for the manufacture of tools for the housewife, and he was connected with several factories in different states; all built irons. The Bless and Drake plant at Newark, N. J. manufactured irons until about 1900. Bless used as a trademark Hephaestus, the Greek god of ironworkers; and the whisk-

ered, hairy head of this ancient god appeared on the dampers of his charcoal irons.

21. Combination smoothing and

fluting iron, ca. 1870, by Bless and Drake, also made by Cummings and Bless. The height of the smokestack was lowered about this time.

The Sensibles

21x. Sensible, patented Sept. 19, 1871, shows early detachable handle.

22. N. R. Streeter & Co., Groton, N. Y. made their Sensible irons in several types for different uses, from at least 1871 to 1908. At left, 1-lb. iron which a hatter used as a tolliker,

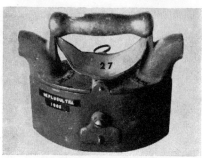

though this size was also used by children and as a salesman's sample. Next, a 7-lb. sad iron dated 1881 on handle; in front of it, a 3-lb. iron, 1871. Right rear, smoothing iron, dated 1908; this has a sheet of asbestos through the center; lower front, a sleeve iron.

23. Sensible sleeve iron, 1888.

24. Sensible smoothing iron, 1908.

25. Hatters' irons, called tollikers or shackles, were used to mellow the hat rims; they came in many shapes and were made by many companies. They took very little heat, and many had wooden handles and handle posts like the two at left, built by M. Mirrer Co., New York, since 1900. Two on right are of a style built for over a hundred years. The lying-down example is all wood, and quite modern.

26. Asbestos Sad Iron, dated 1900. The large one is a smoother; small one, a flounce iron. Removable skirt and handle was lined with asbestos to hold heat from the hand. The Asbestos came in a variety of sets composed of three irons to one handle.

27. "Neplusultra," patented 1902, burned a coke nugget which was sold by its maker, the National Iron Distributing Co., 817 Foss Ave., Drexel Hill, Pa. It was improved and called "Onlyone." Patents were issued in 1914, 1924, and 1932, with slight changes in pattern.

28. Tailor's steam iron, 14-pounds, manufactured by Peth Pressing Process, Buffalo, N. Y., was first patented Sept. 20, 1910. Steam was produced from a boiler, usually in a back room; the finger button released the steam which entered through a hose leading to the larger pipe; the surplus was expelled through the small pipe and carried by the exhaust hose outside the building.

29. The Royal, which burned kerosene; kerosene irons usually have two adjustments.

30. Early Coleman, which burned alcohol, ca. 1900.

31. Hot Point travel iron, by Edison Electric Appliance Co., Inc., patented Feb. 6, 1900 and Aug. 15, 1905, has flat contacts for extension cord. It boiled water, heated two curling irons, and the holder folded into a trivet to hold iron while ironing.

32. Hot Point 20-lb. tailor's iron,

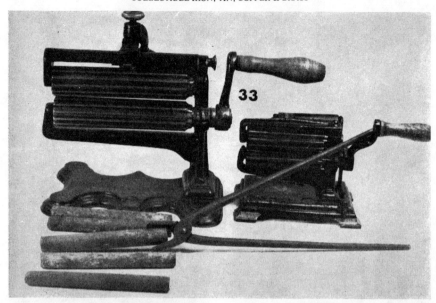

first patented by Edison Electric Appliance Co., June 11, 1910, used 110 volts and had a High, Low, and Off setting on the switch.

33. The large Crown and the smaller Eagle fluting irons were both patented in the 1870s.

35. In earlier days, a Chinese launderer held and blew water from his mouth on the clothes being ironed. Americans frowned on the practice; hence the blow can, about the turn of this century, to be held in the mouth while ironing.

36. Trivet with folding point.

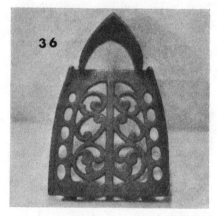

Polishing and Smoothing Irons

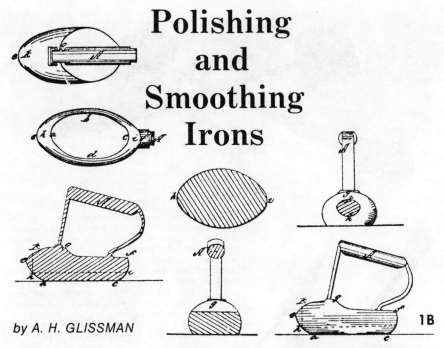

by A. H. GLISSMAN

1B

POLISHING and smoothing irons have been known in England and France since the early 19th century. It is believed that such irons originated in France, but as yet no proof for this premise has been found. Among the irons shown in our illustrations are some made in America in the mid-19th century. The pictures are all from the Glissman collection of irons, one of the largest and finest in the United States, which contains many examples of polishing and smoothing irons.

Figure 1 A: The iron on the left was listed in an 1899 English catalog as a "polisher." The two irons on the right bear the legend "M.A.B. Cook, Pat. 1848" (patented in America by Mary Ann B. Cook, Boston, Mass., December 5, 1848). In her patent papers Mrs. Cook stated that the convex shape of the heel and toe of her iron made it ideal for "smoothing and polishing shirt bosoms." To polish the fabric, the iron was tilted forward on its heavy convex toe; the additional weight at this portion supplied the pressure needed for polishing. The flat surface of the iron, which was thinner, held just the right amount of heat required for smoothing the material.

Figure 1 B: (At Top) Illustrations which accompanied Mrs. Cook's patent papers.

1A

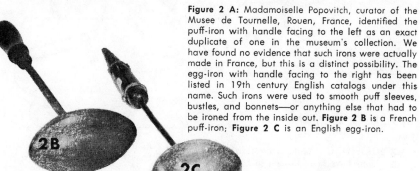

Figure 2 A: Madamoiselle Popovitch, curator of the Musee de Tournelle, Rouen, France, identified the puff-iron with handle facing to the left as an exact duplicate of one in the museum's collection. We have found no evidence that such irons were actually made in France, but this is a distinct possibility. The egg-iron with handle facing to the right has been listed in 19th century English catalogs under this name. Such irons were used to smooth puff sleeves, bustles, and bonnets—or anything else that had to be ironed from the inside out. **Figure 2 B** is a French puff-iron; **Figure 2 C** is an English egg-iron.

Ball-irons (**Figure 3 A**), egg-irons (**Figure 3 B**), and mushroom-irons (**Figures 3 C and 3 D**) were mounted on stands and called "standing irons" in various catalogs. There were many shapes made, each one given a special name to fit the shape. Originally, these irons were heated in hot coals and wiped clean before use; around 1900, steam was used to heat these irons. Electric irons of this type can be purchased today, complete with a stand that clamps onto the ironing board. English catalogs illustrated such irons from the early 1800s to 1925. The early irons weighed from 2 to 8 pounds each; they were used to iron puff sleeves, bustles, and bonnets. The mushroom-iron can be removed from its base and used as a smoother.

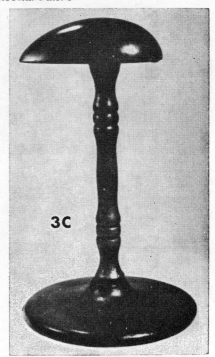

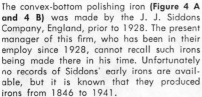

The convex-bottom polishing iron (**Figure 4 A and 4 B**) was made by the J. J. Siddons Company, England, prior to 1928. The present manager of this firm, who has been in their employ since 1928, cannot recall such irons being made there in his time. Unfortunately no records of Siddons' early irons are available, but it is known that they produced irons from 1846 to 1941.

5A

Irons with checkered soles, like those in **Figure 5 A,** were designed to produce the most friction with the least amount of pressure. The most popular shape resembled a hatter's iron. The French style usually has a diamond-patterned corrugated sole like the one shown in the center of **Figure 5 A.** Irons of this design were brought to Mexico by the French during their invasion of that country, in the mid-19th century. When the French were forced to leave Mexico, in 1867, they left behind many of these irons. Consequently, smoothing and polishing irons of this type can be found in Mexico from Guadalajara to Mexico City. Some have the name of the manufacturer on them; others do not; most weigh about 4 pounds.

The iron shown at top center in **Figure 5 A** is marked "M. Mahony, Troy, N.Y." It was patented by Michael Mahony in November 1876 (Pat. No. 184,881). The iron shown at top right in **Figure 5 A** is marked "Geneva" and was made in Geneva, Ill. Another smoothing iron in the author's collection, marked "Genoa," came to him from Genoa, Italy.

5B

The smoothing iron at far left in **Figure 5 A,** and in **Figure 5 B,** has a convex sole and a wrought iron handle; it was made in England in the last half of the 19th century.

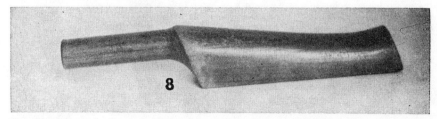

8

The object shown in **Figure 8** (Above) is a cable splicer's tool used to smooth and pound lead around a splice made in a lead covered cable. A tool of this description has recently been incorrectly identified as a smoothing device for pressing and drying damp clothes.

Illustration from Michael Mahoney's patent for an "Improvement in Sad-Irons"; the smooth projections produced the much desired gloss on linens.

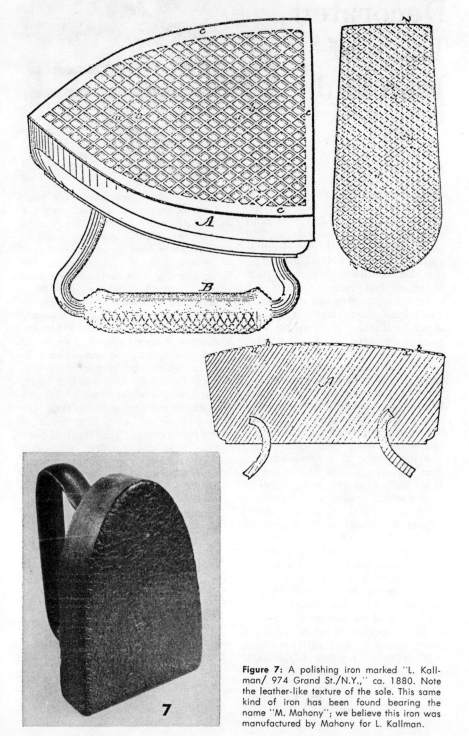

Figure 7: A polishing iron marked "L. Kallman/ 974 Grand St./N.Y.," ca. 1880. Note the leather-like texture of the sole. This same kind of iron has been found bearing the name "M. Mahony"; we believe this iron was manufactured by Mahony for L. Kallman.

Decorated Tools of Iron and Steel

by CARROLL HOPF

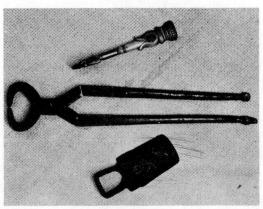

WEBSTER'S DICTIONARY defines the word tool in part as: "Any implement or object used in performing an operation or carrying on work of any kind, esp. where the implement or object is used or worked by hand." One can conclude from this partial definition that there are many different artifacts which may be correctly called tools, from carpenter's planes, chisels, and adzes to finely executed utensils employed by a seamstress for sewing together cloth.

The merit of any tool is quite naturally judged upon its functional value when used in the given task for which it was designed. The functional quality may be analyzed in terms of how well a particular tool withstands the stress and strains encountered when in use, and the quality of the finished task. Here we must assume that a tool, a sharp axe for example, in the hands of a competent person, would perform superior to a dull axe as far as determining the quality of the completed job. Durability and performance, we can say, were and are today the required requisites of a desirable tool. With emphasis placed upon above criteria during the tool making process, whether by hand processes before the advent of the industrial revolution or by mechanical means thereafter, it seems apparent that little emphasis was extended towards superficially decorating tools in general. The seemingly substantial numbers of undecorated tools from both eras which have survived to present day also bear out this statement.

These three tools share one common characteristic in that they are each decorated to some degree. The small wrought iron grubbing hoe (bottom) has a heart motif stamped into the iron. It is only 5¾" long. The farrier's pincers (center), for removing nails from the shoe and hoof of a horse, displays more intricate embellishment consisting of a dog's head and faceted ball at the end of the handles. Farther up each handle it is decorated with fine chisel work. The initials E.M. are stamped into a circular medallion. They supposedly belonged to a blacksmith who worked in Clay, Pennsylvania, in the late 19th century. The pincers are 16" long. The handle of the pastry crimper (top) is carved from bone and displays a tulip motif with cross hatching; the crimping roller is made of iron, while other metal parts are brass. Overall length is 7". Hoe and pincers are from the author's collection; crimper from the collection of The Pennsylvania Farm Museum.

Tools exhibiting some form of decoration — carving, molded or cast,
wrought, punched, stamped, engraved,
or by other means — may be thought
of as reflecting traditional as well as
contemporary cultural values of their
respective periods. As such they be-

*Included in an assortment of tools necessary to carry on
the trade of coppersmithing would have been several stakes
of different shape and size over which sheet copper was
hammered into shape. Today stakes are difficult to locate
on the antique tool market. As numerous as they must have
been, one can only surmise that many were sold for scrap
iron as coppersmiths went out of business. The stamped
decorative pattern and date of 1833 makes this example
particularly interesting. Overall height is 15½". Length is
25". Collection of The Pennsylvania Farm Museum.*

*Of German origin, the flax hetchel is decorated with
geometric motifs incised in the wood with a compass.
Traces of blue and orange remain in the motifs. The hetchel
is an important tool in preparing flax fibers for spinning.
Fibers were first pulled through the iron teeth set farthest
apart. This not only straightened out the fibers but left
coarse strands caught in the teeth. The finest flax thread
was spun from fiber still remaining in the hand after being
pulled through the set of fine teeth. Coarse fiber was spun
into heavy tow material used for sacking.*

*The hetchel is 30½" in length and probably dates from
the first half of the 19th century. Author's collection.*

come valued documents contributing to a better understanding of social and material culture history.

Assembling a collection of decorated tools can be a prolonged experience both interesting and educational. The accompanying photographs illustrate an assortment of embellished tools from agricultural artifacts to sewing items. Comparable examples are yet to be found on the general antiques market. It probably will take some searching to find unusual examples, but after all, isn't that half the enjoyment of antiques collecting.

The broad axe was indispensable for hewing and dressing logs after they had been cut down. It was used with two hands and generally had a handle less than 24" long. Broad axes exist in various form; some examples, as this one (top) have the blade sharpened only on a single side of the axe, hence the term "chisel-edged" blade. Others are sharpened on both sides and are "knife edged." Overall size and shape varies extensively. Broad axes are sometimes found with decorative stamping as this example illustrates. The date 1835 can be seen immediately above the two horizontal grooves. The splitting wedge (bottom) exhibits a particularly unusual stamped design. The patterns on both tools were applied by the use of a hardened metal die with the pattern cut in relief. Overall length of the broad axe is 11"; the wedge is 9½" long. Collection of The Pennsylvania Farm Museum.

Hatchets

by HENRY J. KAUFFMAN

TODAY'S COLLECTORS OF tools are particularly interested in those used for shaping wood; there were many of them, used over a long span of years, and a great number have survived in a remarkable state of preservation. The axe seems to be considered of most importance; it is probably the oldest of tools, and it offers a multitude of variations. One would expect the hatchet to claim like interest and importance because of its similarity in shape and function. But not so!

Tool historians and collectors alike have relegated the hatchet to undeserved obscurity. W. L. Goodman in *The History of Woodworking Tools* did not even include the word in the index to his book. While the hatchet probably reached a higher status in America than in Europe, it was far from unknown there. This writer once discovered a marvelous example on the Left Bank in Paris.

The earliest reference found to the hatchet is in *Mechanicks Exercises* by Moxon, published in 1703. One entry suggests the hatchet was a light tool, basiled (beveled) on one side only, and used with one hand. Continuing evidence through the years indicates that the hatchet was a hewing tool and, at least in earliest times, did not have a facility for pulling nails. Because the inner surfaces of small boards on furniture of the 17th and 18th centuries were finished by hewing, a small tool for such a purpose would have had wide use.

There was doubtless some overlapping in the use of a hatchet and a hand axe. Yet an illustration in *Mechanicks Exercises* shows a tool which clearly resembles a lathing hatchet of modern times. It is called a "Mason's Tool" and described as: "A lathing hammer . . . with which the laths are nailed on with its head, and with its edge they cut them to length, and likewise cut off any part of a quarter *(sic)* or joyst, that stick further out than the rest."

Thus it is evident that at the beginning of the 18th century the tool was used for both nailing and splitting. The lathing hatchet pictured with the above description was narrow so that it could be used to drive nails in the corner made by the ceiling and the side wall. Its function as a hewing tool can be discerned since one side of the tool is flat, the bulge of the handle being entirely on the opposite side.

An example of a similar tool, but with a canted handle, is in this author's collection. Mercer does not mention this type in describing the hatchet in his *Ancient Carpenter's Tools*. Possibly due to the often small nature of its work, it did not require such a handle. While Mercer's description confirms that there were hewing hatchets, most of the nine which he illustrates appear to be small axes.

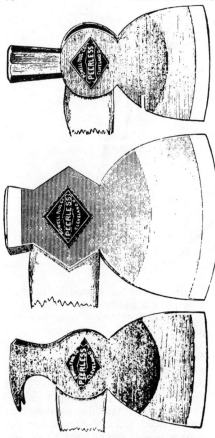

Illustrations from the tool catalog of T. B. Rayl & Co. of Detroit, Mich., probably dating late 19th century. These focus attention on different styles of hatchets. Most of the claw type were manufactured in the late 19th century and early 20th century.

The hewing hatchet in this author's collection was made by welding two slabs of iron together and edging the bit with a piece of steel. This procedure was followed because iron was cheap and easily welded, both properties lacking in steel. After the steel edge was ground away from many sharpenings, a new piece was "laid" on the edge, providing an adequate tool for many more years of use.

Also in regard to the hatchet used as a hewing tool, *The Cyclopedia: or Universal Dictionary of Arts and Sciences,* by E. Chambers, published in London in 1751, reads: "HATCHET: a joiner's instrument wherewith to hew wood.

The hatchet is a smaller, lighter sort of ax, with a basil edge on its left side; having a short handle, as being to be used with one hand."

In 1753, a *Supplement* of the same publication gives other uses for the tool. It is the only reference found which suggests its use as a weapon. "HATCHET (cycl) a small ax, used by pioneers, who go before to prepare the ways for an army, by cutting down hedges, bushes, styles, or gates. The grenadiers carry some times a hatchet by their side; and French dragoons, who have but one pistol, have a hatchet hanging at their saddle-bows, on the right side."

The hatchet was always a one-handed tool, but its modern function as a household and carpenter utility tool was unknown in the 18th century. Mercer says of it: "While the larger broad axe held its own through the 19th century, this little, basiled, one-handed tool, with or without a pounding poll, owing to the increased abundance of ready-prepared lumber dressed in the planing mills, fell out of use after 1830, while two other forms of the hatchet, used for rough-surfacing, splitting, chopping, and nailing, became more and more the continual companions of the carpenter."

A 19th century form of the hatchet, not recognized by Mercer but illustrated in the business catalog of T. B. Rayl & Co. of Detroit, is the half hatchet. It had less spread in the bit than the full shingling hatchet but more than the narrow lathing hatchet. Mercer evidently never made this distinction since he classes the half hatchet with the lathing type.

Although half hatchets are not a common form, some at least were made in the 1860s and 1870s by Beatty who worked in Chester, Pennsylvania, and had a salesroom in Philadelphia. As a trademark he used his name, "Beatty," and an impressed representation of a cow. Often the cow was so lightly impressed that it is difficult to find.

The full shingling hatchet is the tool most people envision when the word "hatchet" is mentioned today. Among the examples pictured here is one with an intaglio impression of two undecipherable letters. It has a contracted head for driving nails, and a slit in the bit

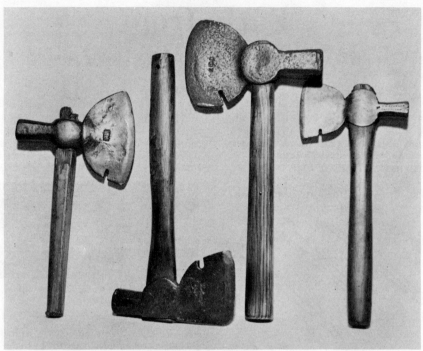

Four hatchets of interest to the tool collector. The first on the left is a so-called shingling hatchet with an intaglio stamped mark which cannot be deciphered. The second is a half-hatchet with the name "Beatty" and the outline of a cow impressed in the metal. The third is marked "C. Kidd" who worked in Baltimore in the second quarter of the 19th century. The last one is marked "C. W. Bradley" whose location is not known; this latter tool was purchased in Connecticut.

to pull nails. It is made of iron and on its edge was "laid" a piece of steel for cutting purposes.

The *Index of Patents,* issued from the U. S. Patent Office from 1790 to 1873, lists only six patents granted for hatchets while more than one hundred were issued for axes. Although there seems no clear cut difference between a hatchet and a small hand axe, a hatchet, generally speaking is a small tool, designed for use with one hand, with a contracted stud or poll for driving nails and a facility for pulling nails. Considerable research remains to be done before the hatchet story is completely told.

Early Iron Hardware

by RAYMOND F. YATES

HARDWARE is a guide to dating old furniture, and the collector should learn to recognize the nails, screws, hinges, drawer pulls, and the like used on truly old pieces.

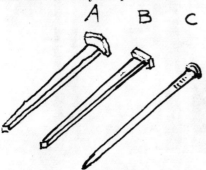

A, old crude hand-forged square nail, 1700-1800; B, machine-cut nail, 1810-1890; C, modern wire nail.

NAILS: The earliest nails used in both house and furniture construction were hand-forged, and were usually made by "nailers" who worked at home. These square nails were forged, one by one, from high purity "Russian iron," which did not rust. About 1830, nails were made by machine; these, too, were square. Since square nails were used as late as the 1880s, when the modern round nail was introduced, the sight of a square nail-head on a piece of furniture is not convincing proof that the piece is old.

Really old square nails are much cruder than the machine product. The blanks had to be heated, then shaped and headed. Hand-forged nails show hammer and anvil marks; the surfaces are rough; the heads are anything but perfectly square or oblong. They rusted very little, while machine-made nails rusted badly. If the collector carefully examines old hand-forged nails, he will quickly learn to recognize them. Such nails were used only on primitive pieces, mostly of pine. Early cabinetmakers who worked for the carriage trade did not use nails.

SCREWS: The removal of a screw and careful inspection of it by the collector—a small magnifying glass is helpful—will often help him date a piece of furniture. The crude hand-made wood screws used before 1830

Old hand-filed screws with blunt points; some were used to 1830s.

are easily identified. The spiral threads are hand-cut with a three-cornered file; the slots on the screw heads are shallow and often badly off center; the ends are blunt instead of sharply pointed. To start the screw into the wood, a hole was made by a gimlet. The blunt-ended wood screw was inserted into it and driven home with a screw driver. Modern sharp-pointed, perfectly uniform, machine-made "gimlet screws" began to be manufactured during the 1840s by the American Screw Company. While the presence of hand-filed screws usually means a piece of furniture is a real antique, furniture fakers have been known to switch screws in an effort to fool experts.

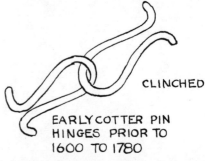

CLINCHED

EARLY COTTER PIN HINGES PRIOR TO 1600 TO 1780

HINGES: Hinges vary a great deal. The earliest forms appeared in New England on blanket chest lids. Some were no more than pieces of cowhide nailed in place. Such leather hinges are difficult to date; farmers have used them for years. Cotter pin hinges, also used on pine blanket chest lids, were made with iron wire, and can be as easily reproduced with a piece of modern iron wire as leather hinges can be replaced with an old bit of harness. Blanket chests with original cotter pin hinges are rare.

Butterfly and rattail hinges, hand-wrought by blacksmiths, were used during the eighteenth and early nine-teenth centuries. Rattail hinges were usually employed on blanket chest lids. Similar hinges were manufac-tured from the 1840s through the 1860s, the machine-made hinges being smooth with no hammer marks. How-ever, one must remember that modern

The H and HL hinges were made in brass as well as iron. From 1760 to 1800, brass hardware was seldom used on anything but formal carriage-trade furniture. It was imported from England until the Revolution. After that, local craftsmen began to copy it for use on mahogany pieces in the Chippendale, Hepplewhite and Adams styles which they were creating from English design books.

Sharp accurate screw threads on modern machine-cut bolt; crude threads made by hand with a file, before 1830.

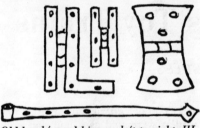

Old hand-forged hinges: left to right, HL, H, butterfly; below, rattail.

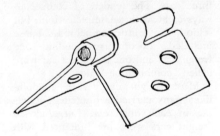

HAND-FORGED HINGES 1725-1800

HAND MADE DRAW PULL POST - BRASS 1750 - 1820

hinges alone do not date a piece; worn-out hinges could have been re-placed by original owners. Instances are known where an early owner had himself removed fine brass hardware to install a set of later Sandwich glass knobs.

DRAWER PULLS: Some of the earliest drawer pulls were lathe-turned wooden knobs. These cannot be classed as hardware unless they were attached with wood screws, which have their own story to tell as to date. Many wooden knobs or pulls were held to the drawer front with a dowel pin glued in place; these are usually early ones, although this is not a posi-tive clue to dating. All screws and bolts used to hold early metal drawer pulls to drawer fronts were hand-cut. The screws with their crude threads are especially easy to recognize.

"Cannon Ball Train," the largest iron toy train made by Ives, Blakeslee and Williams Company, in 1893.

"Michigan Central R.R.," a scarce nickle-plated iron toy train believed to have been made by either the Kenton Hardware Company, Kenton, Ohio, or the Grey Iron Company, Reading, Pennsylvania (?), ca. 1910.

Iron Trackless Toy Trains

by EMMA STILES

WIDELY SOUGHT BY COLLECTORS today are the trackless iron toy trains which first appeared in America in the late 1870s. These trackless trains were string-pulled, hand-pushed, or mechanical, the mechanical locomotives housing a strong clockwork movement.

Made of cast, as well as malleable iron—the malleable being earlier and most rare — locomotives and molded cars were cast in lengthwise sections. Molten metal was poured into sand molds, which were removed when the metal had cooled and solidified. Joining the seams, adding the axle and wheels completed the car.

The first iron trains were rather stiff in style, more or less copied from earlier tin types; many were virtually scale models. From 1880 to 1890, they grew more refined and more elaborate. They continued to flourish up to about 1930. By then, the models were generally smaller and less detailed.

Locomotives were sold individually, as were extra large freight and passenger cars, measuring more than 17 inches long, and wholesaled in 1893 at $13.50 per dozen. Locomotives and tenders were sold as a unit; but most often the complete train consisted of locomotive, tender, and one, two, or three cars. The tender, of course, always came with a complete train, but seldom was a little tag-behind caboose included. Locomotives pulling one freight car and one passenger car were called "combination trains."

Most freight cars were gondola-like; many carried a brakeman standing in each open car. Large closed freight cars were manufactured with movable side doors; these are considered rare today. Vestibule, observation, and passenger cars were also made.

The Wilkins Toy Company of Keene, N. H., in their 1911 toy catalog advertised "coal freight trains"— locomotive, tender, and one, two, or three coal cars. These were enameled, embossed, and decorated. "P.R.R." in high raised gold letters covered the entire sides of each coal car. A movement of lever to either side of the coal car opened swinging doors in the bottom, allowing the load to dump;

returning lever to normal position closed the doors.

The terms of the Wilkins Toy Co. stated "All shipments F.O.B." They made no allowance for breakage, nor guaranteed delivery. Their goods were packed in regular crates or cases as specified and if ordered differently or in less quantity, a higher price would be charged for special handling. Of the 32 trains in their 1911 catalog, only two included a caboose.

Ehrich Brothers, Eighth Avenue, New York, N. Y., advertised in their 1882 winter mail order catalog a solid iron toy train—locomotive, tender, and two freight cars, painted red and black, packed in a sliding-cover wooden box at 95 cents, but stated shipment would be made by express.

The Ives, Blakeslee and Williams Company, 294 Broadway, New York City, whose factory was in Bridgeport, Conn., displayed a most attractive line of iron toy trains in their 1893 toy catalog. Locomotives had been included in the Ives toy production since the 1870s. The Ives company was the great pioneer in the iron toy field and where it led, others followed. Competitive imitations, lacking the finer detail and castings of the Ives models, appeared a year or two after Ives introduced some new toy.

In their 1893 catalog, Ives introduced an entirely new and original steel passenger train with observation car. It was 58 inches long; the locomotive and tender were iron and japanned black; the passenger coaches were of steel and painted in brilliant colors.

In the same catalog, Ives advertised their new model, the "Cannon Ball Train," the largest iron train made, with locomotive, tender, closed freight car and vestibule car. The number "189" was embossed in an oblong panel on both sides of the tender; "Union/*/Line/*" was embossed on the right front side of the freight car, and "Capacity 50,000 pounds" on the back side. The decoration was reversed on the opposite side. Printed in raised letters on the passenger car were the words, "Limited Vestibule Express." Despite its lettering, the passenger car was of the non-vestibule design. The locomotive was an extremely accurate representation of the real thing. The details on it extended to tiny bolt heads, cast on the side rods. When coupled together as a unit, this large cast iron trackless pull-train measured almost five feet long. It wholesaled at $54 per dozen. Three trains, packed for shipping in a wooden crate, 13 x 20 x 32 inches, weighed 104 pounds.

Another special train advertised by Ives that year was the celebrated White Train or Ghost Train, 41 inches long—

The manufacturer (s) of these iron toy trains could not be identified, but they are typical of the types made in the late 19th century and can be found in various sizes.

"Baltimore & Ohio" iron toy train attributed to the Wilkins Toy Company, ca. 1900.

locomotive, tender, and two white vestibule cars. It wholesaled at $21 per dozen; one dozen. packed in a crate. weighed 198 pounds.

The least expensive four-unit passenger train in the Ives 1893 catalog was called "The Hero." It was 14 inches long and sold at $4 per dozen. The least expensive four-unit freight sold at $2 a dozen; it, too, was 14 inches long. Of the 13 complete trains displayed in their 1893 catalog, not one showed a caboose.

The Carpenter Line of Toys catalog, a 5x7 inch, 22-page, paper-cover pamphlet, reprinted by F. A. O. Schwarz of New York for the Antique Toy Collectors Club, carried a good selection of iron trains. Though the date of the original catalog is not given, patent dates appear under each picture. One freight train listed five patents and re-issue dates between May 4, 1880, and May 13, 1884. The name Williard & McKee, 21 Park Place, New York City, presumably the distributors, appeared on the front cover of the catalog.

There is some mystery in connection with the Carpenter toys, for no one yet has been able to pin down a manufacturer's name or address for them. Apparently Carpenter farmed out his work. Patent No. 227216 for a toy train was issued to Francis W. Carpenter at Rye, N. Y., on May 4, 1880, and Patent No. 298446, for a toy railroad, to Francis W. Carpenter at Harrison, N. Y., on May 13, 1884.

Of the five complete trains displayed in the Carpenter catalog, not one came with a caboose.

The Hubley Manufacturing Company, Lancaster, Pa., in their 1906 catalog, advertised train "No. 60-½"— locomotive, tender, and two passenger cars, polished copper oxidized." It weighed over 12 pounds and was 43 inches long. There were 14 complete trains shown in the Hubley catalog; of these only three pulled a caboose.

The most desirable of the early iron locomotives, aside from the very large pieces, are 2-2-0 models, lettered "Big Six" or bearing the patent dates May 4, 1880, May 25, 1880, June 8, 1880, Aug. 16, 1881, or Aug. 19, 1884. Models bearing these patent dates were manufactured until about 1900 by J. & E. Stevens Co., Cromwell, Conn., as well as by others.

Of the 1915 period, the largest size cars, 15 inches or more in length, any of the model street cars, and the iron electric-type locomotive are the most desirable.

The little locomotives with the tender cast integral and only one pair of movable wheels were staple designs in virtually every line for more than 40 years and are quite common. To entice children to play with the trains, parents called, "Johnnie, come pull the puffers." The subsequent puffing noise that was heard issued not from the train but from its proud owner's pursed lips.

Cast Iron Fire-Fighting Toys

by MARCIA RAY

THE ARCHIE Stiles family collects just about everything—antique baby buggies, horse prints, old post cards, horse-drawn sleighs and carriages, beer steins, powder flasks, old banks, and shaving mugs. They even have a complete antique barber shop. On their place in Meyersville, New Jersey, they keep an antiques shop, a museum, and a pet farm, too, with tame deer to pull carriages, a trained rooster, and ponies.

Among their favorite collectibles are their iron toys, and they are especially proud of their fire-fighting equipment.

Cast iron fire-fighting toys, when they came on the scene in the 1870s, were comparatively plain. Through the 1880s, they became more elaborate and extraordinarily realistic. Many fire-fighting toys were scale size; some measured almost 3 feet long. Hitches were made with one, two, and three horses; some horses could be unhitched from their shafts. Various

means were taken to provide a galloping motion for the horses. Some horses were made whose four legs moved independently of each other when the toy was pulled along. Fine quality engines carried miniature removable axes, water buckets, and an extra supply of ladders.

Toys Illustrated

The five toys pictured —Fire Chief Wagon, Hose Reel, Steam Pumper, Fire Patrol Wagon, Hook and Ladder — were featured in the 1893 catalog of Ives, Blakeslee & Williams Co., 294 Broadway, New York, whose factory was at Bridgeport, Connecticut.

Featured also was the Mechanical Fire Engine House, an exciting handsome toy with a powerful clock movement. The entire front of the house was made of cast iron, as were the windows and cornice. The roof, floor,

Toys from Ives, Blakeslee & Williams Co., advertised in their 1893 catalog.

and sides were of wood. It measured 8½x12x15½ inches, and wholesaled at $5. The clock motor was set above the doors on the inside front of the house. The directions were to "wind as you would a clock; pull out the stop wire on outer side of the house; after the bell has struck one-two, one-two, three, the doors fly open and the engine dashes for the fire."

The sides of the Chief's Wagon, drawn by galloping horses, were covered with bold embossed letters, reading CHIEF. The Hose Reel carriage had four wheels; hose reel carts were made with two. The hitches consisted of one, two, or three running horses; realistic hose was wrapped round and round the free turning reel.

The Steam Pumper, a mechanical fire engine with racing horses, 5x7x19 inches, was made with a clock motor. When wound, the two small wheels in front of the boiler and the pump work rapidly, imitating an engine at work. These sold in 1893 at $36 per dozen, wholesale.

The Fire Patrol Wagon — with a driver on the front, and 6 cast iron firemen in uniform sitting on the side benches, ready to leap out at the first sign of smoke — had an embossed FIRE PATROL, covering both side panels. The Hook and Ladder, with running horses pulling the Hook and Ladder truck, carried driver, tillerman, and ladders.

The company also advertised in this same catalog a "great new addition to the toy fire brigade — two iron extension ladders, 18 inches long, 4 cast iron firemen in bright uniforms, and one length of rubber hose with nozzle, packed in a neat box." It wholesaled at $5 per dozen.

Kicking Cow: Press flower-shaped lever and cow flips tail, kicks stool, farmer with bucket lands on back in grass. Product of Stevens Foundry, Cromwell, Conn. (1888).

Mechanical Iron Banks

by WILLIAM H. MONTGOMERY

A NTIQUE mechanical banks have long been collectors' items. Today they are being so assiduously sought by bankers and financial institutions as well as established collectors that the casual collector may find them so scarce as to seem almost unobtainable. Prices, too, have spiralled to such fantastic heights as to discourage the newcomer from the thought of acquiring a sizable collection. However, at least *one* antique bank, either a good mechanical or a good still, is within range of every

Bad Accident: Lever operates mechanism to send boy leaping from behind bush to frighten mule and upset cart with watermelon-eating farmer. As wagon falls, boy retreats, coin under wagon seat falls in body of wagon.

collector's purse and province and belongs in every over-all collection of Americana.

These banks, which reached their height of popularity in the 1870s and 1880s, though some were made earlier, and others as late as 1915, were primarily toys rather than objects for the encouragement of thrift. Nearly all of them can be operated by pressing the lever or knob without the necessity of depositing a coin. Because most of the banks were of iron, shatterable if dropped, it is no wonder that a majority of those manufactured have been broken. The chipped and worn paint on many remaining attest to hard use through the years.

A large part of the charm of these old banks stems from the fact that they are pure Americana. Even the substance of which they were manufactured, iron, was not plentiful enough in other countries to be used in children's toys. However, iron foundries in the United States found toys profitable, and employed really good artists to design the banks and plan the concealed mechanisms which made the parts move. The designers used many familiar figures in their choice of subject. Banks appeared featuring such typically American sports as baseball, football and bowling, or such popular types of entertainment as magicians, Punch & Judy Shows, performing animals, and acrobats. They ranged from a Preacher in the Pulpit bank to popular comic strip characters, like Uncle Remus, the Katzenjammer Kids and the "Shoot the Chutes" bank with Buster Brown and Tige.

Many of them portray a raucous humor, with people getting into accidents, often with animals as the cause of the trouble. Butting goats, kicking cows, bucking mules and buffalo provided slapstick comedy. The animals are generally well-proportioned and pleasing to the eye, and the people, lovable and good-humored, never seemed to mind much when they are knocked over to stand on their heads or lie flat on their backs. Often the exaggerated facial expressions are very funny. The old bank designers, in their zeal to make the children laugh, created masterpieces of humor which have fascinated generations of adults as well.

Always Did 'Spise A Mule: Grinning jockey holds coin in mouth, press of lever pitches him forward over mule's head, depositing penny in base of bank. Upside down gr'n seems to become expression of pain (1879)

The prices of old mechanical banks vary a great deal depending on their rarity. While the "Kicking Cow" and "Always Did 'Spise a Mule" are perhaps equally attractive and similar in action, the "Kicking Cow" is much more rare. John D. Meyer's book, copyright in 1952, prices this " 'Spise a Mule" bank at $22, and the Kicking Cow bank at $200!

The Dentist bank, pictured, was originally sold by the manufacturer for $8 a dozen. The selling price listed by Ina Hayward Bellows in her *Old Mechnical Banks,* published in 1940, was between $20 and $30 each. In 1952, John D. Meyer in his *Handbook of Old Mechanical Penny Banks,* set the current price at $165. In April, 1955, a catalogue published by David Hollander, New York, offering for sale a number of mechanical and still banks from the Chrysler Collection, listed the same bank, in fine condition, with original paint at $350. It is a safe guess that today's spiralling prices will seem low to a future generation.

In the parlance of the trade, "O.P." means "Original Paint" and "O.F.," "Original Finish." A bank is said to be in "mint" condition if it still has all

Dentist: A penny slipped into dentist's pocket as he stands poised for action, and a press of lever, sends him backward, tooth in forceps, while coin flips into gas bag. Simultaneously patient and chair tip backward.

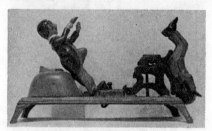

quantities. Some of the rarest of all are ones which a manufacturer put on the market only to find he could not sell them advantageously and withdrew the model after a comparatively small number had been made.

Magician: Theatrical figure, on platform labelled Magician Bank, at operation of lever, lowers hat over coin placed on table. When hat is raised, coin has disappeared through magician's legs to base of platform. (1882)

or virtually all of its original paint. Of course, a bank which is "mint" is worth more than the same bank in a badly faded condition, or with much of the paint gone or badly chipped. However, most collectors want nothing whatever to do with a bank that has been repainted. Hence an old bank, even with little or none of its original paint left is more valuable than if repainted. Many repaint jobs are crude in both conception and execution, but even the most expert restorer, bent on deception, would find it as hard to repaint a bank in the original colors to fool a connoisseur of banks as to counterfeit money to deceive a Treasury man.

Non-experts who contemplate buying a mechanical bank would do well to seek the advice of experienced bank collectors in order to avoid the pitfalls of buying a repainted job, worth, perhaps, only a fraction of the price asked, or of paying a too high a price for one of the less rare banks.

It is to be remembered that some of the most attractive mechanical banks are the cheapest because they were immensely popular and sold in the largest numbers. Rarer banks may be those which were more fragile, or ones with less popular appeal which were manufactured in small

Mammy & Child: Originally advertised as Baby Mine: Baby kicks as Mammy feeds coin placed on spoon into outsized mouth of child. Will swallow up to 25¢ piece. Second slot in Mammy's apron is unusual feature. (1884)

Collectible Still Banks

by WILLIAM H. MONTGOMERY

(Photos by Doris Montgomery)

PENNY banks of pottery, glass and tin appeared early on the American scene. Poor Richard's adage "A penny saved is a penny earned" was taken quite literally, and as soon as the first copper pennies were minted in 1793, enterprising glassmakers and potters had banks ready to hold them.

Sometime after 1860, cast iron banks appeared. Though a few still banks in iron antedate the mechanical banks, it was not until the late 19th and early 20th centuries that the still bank achieved mass popularity.

That many of these still banks are scarcely fifty years old seems not to detract from their interest to today's collectors, but rather to add by this very "lateness" a certain nostalgic charm. Makers of still banks, as of the mechanicals, turned to the fads and fancies of the day for inspiration, and it was not so long ago that Black Beauty was on every bookshelf, the Flatiron Building was the place to see in New York, Mutt and Jeff were in the Sunday funnies, and performing animals made Circus Day memorable. Iron still banks, cast in such pleasant molds appeal both to those who "remember when" and to those whose "Grandma had one!"

Earlier still banks were usually of two pieces of metal, bolted or screwed together, to be opened by removing bolts or screws. Around 1895, safe and building banks appeared, which were opened by working a combination on the door. This type was popular as late as the 1920s.

Many attractive forms are being currently issued by banks and thrift institutions which reflect today's interests. One such features an airplane, others Daniel Boone, David Crockett, Captain Kidd and such.

The modest collector, with a fascination for the America of the past seventy-five years and an eye to a collection that is due to increase in

value, may well find it profitable to follow the familiar slogan "America Banks on Banks".

From the funnies, *Mutt and Jeff, Mama Katzenjammer* and her incorrigible boys were popular subjects. Best known of the many famous building banks is *New York's Flatiron Building. Rough Rider Teddy Roosevelt*, about to charge San Juan Hill, is earlier and more difficult to find than a Trick pony bank, for instance, but still attainable. *Black Beauty*, is now one of the rare still banks. So is the *Liberty Bell*, patented 1875, and sold at the Philadelphia Centennial. Printed history, pasted on wood base, describes it as "Bailey's Centennial Money Bank."

Ornamental Iron Works

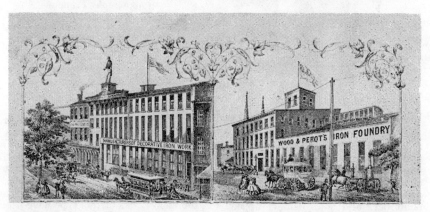

THE rarity of any print has many aspects. Take the above lithograph by Ketterlinus of Philadelphia. It measures only 7 x 4¼ inches, but is packed—literally packed—with important historic information. And this is the story it tells: The Wood & Perot Iron Foundry of Philadelphia sold so much ornamental ironwork to New Orleans customers they erected a branch foundry in the Louisiana Metropolis. That New Orleans foundry is pictured at the right of the print; the Philadelphia works on the left. At both foundries the following items were manufactured: Iron railings for cemetery enclosures, public Squares, Churches, and Private Residences. Iron Verandahs, Balconies, Bank Counters, Stairs (in every variety), Mausoleums, or Tombs, Chairs, Settees, Tables, Tree Boxes, Hitching Posts, Lamp Posts, Brackets, Statuary and all other Iron Work of Decorative Character. Drawings were furnished to those who wish to make selections.

The view of the New Orleans factory of Wood, Miltenberger & Co., shows the Cathedral spires in the background and a steam fire-engine, dray and omnibus on the street. The Philadelphia Foundry, with its gigantic iron statue, is pictured on its Ridge Avenue facade, with the double track horse-car line. The next time you admire the iron lace of the Vieu Carre, chances are you'll be admiring ironwork made at both Philadelphia and New Orleans by the same company. The New Orleans foundry was set up over a century ago.

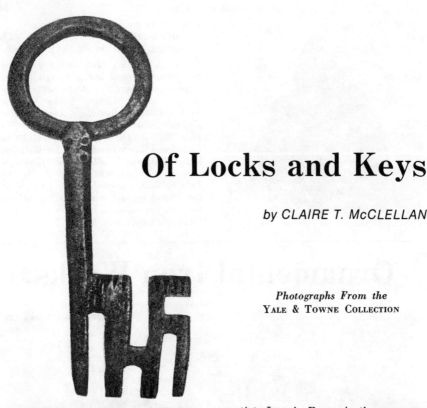

Of Locks and Keys

by CLAIRE T. McCLELLAN

Photographs From the
YALE & TOWNE COLLECTION

I N MOST developing civilizations there comes a time when a stone rolled before a cave, a thong tied to a doorpost, or the recitation of an incantation no longer serves as adequate protection for man's person or accumulating possessions. At this point bars and bolts usually appear. There remains the problem of securing these so that no one but the owner may have access to the property, and locks and keys supply the answer. Evidence that man has met this need in similar ways has been found in the remains of early cultures in many parts of the world—though the results have differed greatly in appearance.

Lock historians agree that the first key-operated locks were probably those in use in the Nile Valley, 4,000 years ago. Such a device was pictured in temple frescoes at Karnak. The earliest actual example of this "Egyptian type" of lock and key was unearthed at the site of the palace of Sargon, near the Biblical city of Nineveh, during the excavations in Asia Minor in the mid-19th century. Its finder, the Italian archeologist-

artist Joseph Bonomi, the younger, described the great wooden lock, and said that its key was "as much as a man can conveniently carry." Such keys somewhat resemble oversize wooden toothbrushes, the "bristles" being pegs to lift falling tumblers in the lock. Locks of this type have been used until very recent times in Mediterranean countries and are still to be found in rural areas.

The huge bronze keys slung over the shoulders of Homeric Greeks were little more than hooks to lift the door bolts, but the Greeks made a significant contribution to lock development by placing these bolts inside the door and using a keyhole.

Among the Romans, lock development progressed rapidly. Skilled metal workers, familiar with all the locking mechanisms then extant, they perfected several designs and made much use of movable locks with keys small enough to be worn as finger-rings. Keys were often given Roman brides to signify their rights to household possessions, a custom surviving for centuries in Europe.

The iron locks of Rome went with

the Legions wherever they carried the Roman standard, but little remains of them except their bronze hasps, bolts and keys, which have not succumbed to rust. Keys in particular have been found in numbers, partly because the cult of the Persian god Mithras was a popular one among the Legionnaires (100-400 A.D.) and one of its rites was the burial of a key with the dead. When Vesuvius covered Pompeii in ashes in 64 A.D., a locksmith's shop was preserved for future study. In it were found doorlocks, padlocks, ornamented keys, and what appears to be a "skeleton" key.

The latter was probably for the smith's use on *warded* locks, introduced into Roman culture by the Etruscans. These are locks in which obstructions or "wards" are placed within the lock, and the key bit has to be cut to pass them in order for

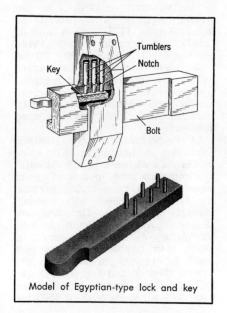

Model of Egyptian-type lock and key

the bolt to be retracted. This type of mechanism became the prototype of European locks for many centuries. All of us are familiar with warded locks, since they are still in use where security is not too essential.

Medieval metalwork is famous for its great beauty, and locksmiths' guilds were exacting. An apprentice was forced to spend ten years before submitting the "masterpiece" that, accepted, would qualify him as a

journeyman. W e a l t h y merchants, bankers, and nobles spent great sums on locks and keys. It is said that Henry II of France had a series of locks made for the apartments of his mistress, each with its own key, while he alone held the "master key" to unlock them all! The lacy heraldic designs of locking devices became more and more elaborate; and a key— sometimes of precious metal — was thought a suitable gift for a monarch to bestow on a favored subject.

Dr. Williamson, in *The Amateur Collector,* published in 1924, tells of a Countess in the reign of the Stuarts, Lady Anne Clifford, who kept a local smith constantly employed fashioning locks for her to give friends, favorite tenants, and local churches. Some of these great rectangular locks with their keys bearing the countess' initials and date were still in use at the time of the book's publication.

Medieval and Renaissance locks were usually ponderous. Great iron keys unlocked dungeons; brass ones with vintage motifs were favored for wine cellars. The chatelaine of manor

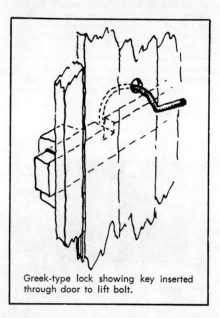

Greek-type lock showing key inserted through door to lift bolt.

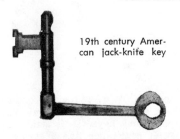

19th century American jack-knife key

or castle carried a ring of keys at her belt for linen press, storeroom, chest, and cabinet—and to give visible evidence of her station in life. Locks were generally too costly for the poor, who had little to protect in any case.

While appearing formidable, European warded locks were fairly easy for the skilled "picker" to open. To foil these, locksmiths came up with dummy and hidden keyholes and with trick devices that might alarm the household with bell or explosion, or even trap, brand, or shoot the would-be thief tampering with the lock. In spite of these precautions and the severe punishment meted out to thieves, lockpicking continued.

Occasionally European lockmakers had added a lever tumbler to the warded locks, but it was not until the latter part of the 18th and early 19th centuries that several English locksmiths invented devices of far greater security. The patents of Robert Barron (1778), Joseph Bramah (1784), and Jeremiah Chubb (1818) are especially noteworthy. These locks, while much safer than warded locks, were complicated, very expensive, and practical only where great wealth was involved or security essential. All locks at this time were handmade.

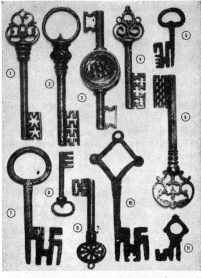

Gothic, Renaissance, and Baroque keys, all for warded locks. **1.** 17th century German cabinet key. **2.** 16th century German cabinet key. **3.** 16th century German passage door key. **4.** 17th century German cabinet key. **5.** 8th century Merovingian cabinet key. **6.** 17th century German passage door key. **7.** 10th century German pasage door key. **8.** 15th century German cabinet key. **9.** 16th century North Italian cabinet key. **10.** 13th-14th century Austrian passage door key. **11.** 8th century Frankish cabinet key.

At the time of the Crystal Palace Exposition in London in 1851, locksmiths on both sides of the Atlantic had come up with models of great ingenuity, and were trying to pick one another's devices with varying degrees of success. Dr. Andrews (Solomon Andrews, Perth Amboy, New Jersey, ca. 1836) had a model in which both tumblers and key bits could be rearranged at will. Mr. Newell (Newell and Day, New York, 1850) made a successful key-operated bank lock after his offer of $500 for

18th cent. prison lock, wards and spring lever mechanism.

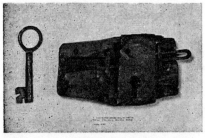

Semi-mortise passage door lock, 17th century.

Lock placed on the West Gate of the Holy Sepulchre in Jerusalem by the Crusaders in 1099 A.D.

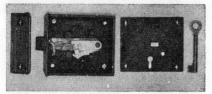

Multiple lever Chubb-type, ca. 1863

Linus Yale, Jr's early pin-tumbler cylinder lock of the 1860s.

anyone able to pick an earlier model had been won. Thousands of patents for locks and improvements were taken out from the time of the American Revolution until the 1920s; some are more interesting than practical. Many of them, however, incorporate the principles in general use today.

A noteworthy example is that of Linus Yale Sr., a maker of bank locks. In 1844, he patented a household cylinder lock, embodying the old "Egyptian" pin-tumblers mechanism. His son, Linus Yale Jr., originally an artist, perfected this in patents of 1861 and 1865, adapting it to the machine production methods coming into use in the industrial age. He formed a partnership with an engineer, Henry Towne, but died just before the formal opening of the factory of the company that still bears his name.

Other early firms, some still in business, are Evans and Watson, Philadelphia, 1852; Russwin, New Britain, Connecticut; and Sargent and Company of New Haven, Connecticut, which celebrated its 100th birthday recently.

American ingenuity and production methods have discouraged foreign competition in our own country, and American locks are an important export item. An Ilco-Lockwood model (Fitchburg, Massachusetts) went with Sir Edmund Hillary to the top of Mt. Everest; and an unusual recent photograph shows an African chieftan wearing very large and heavy padlocks made by the Master Lock Company of Milwaukee as earrings.

"Old Western Jail Keys" from Coryell County, Texas, Jail, built 1875. Largest, 6" long, for front door; next largest for back door; smallest for strongbox; others for cell padlocks. All are Chubb-type.

Collection: Jim Miller, Gatesville, Texas

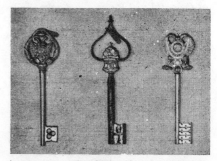

Large, ornate Chamberlain keys, presented by European rulers to court officials, 16th century on. Key at left was given Maria Theresa of Austria. Today we still give visiting dignitaries "a key to the city."

Masterpieces, left to right—Rim lock, 16th cent., French; keyhole cover and left mortise opened by pressing button in lintel. Lock with 4 bolts, 18th cent., French. Door lock, brass plate engraved in German: "Invented and made into a masterpiece by Johann George Popp, 1756, Furth, Germany." To qualify as locksmiths, apprentices submitted masterpieces such as these—after ten years or more of training.

Padlocks were made by both the early Chinese and the Romans. The former seem to have been the innovators of the keyless or "combination" padlock, in which a series of manipulations is necessary to free the hasp. This principle was introduced into Europe around the 16th century, and is still used on safes, vaults, and some modern padlocks.

The derivation of the word "padlock" has been the subject of speculation. Webster's *New World Dictionary* attributes it to the Middle English "padde" or frog, as suggested by the shape of some locks; others have suggested it comes from the attempts to foil the "footpads" or "pads", Medieval thieves. The latter view seems more reasonable, considering the numbers of Oriental and Roman padlocks made in the shape of fish, birds, animals, and mythological figures.

The literature of locks and keys is extensive, containing hundreds of volumes of many dates and in many languages. Some notable libraries of them have been formed; best known are those Mr. William McInerney, the Historian of the Associated Locksmiths of America, and Mr. Robert Nelson of the Mercer Lock Company of Philadelphia, who also has an extensive collection of antique locking devices. A book recommended for the average collector is *The Story of Locks* by Walter Buehr (Chas. Scrib-ner's Sons, 1953), whose readable text and charming illustrations by the author give insight into both the working and history of locks.

All collectors should endeavor to see the traveling exhibits of the famous Yale and Towne Collection, which includes many noteworthy collections acquired by this pioneer American firm. They are booked through the American Federation of Arts, and the public relations department.

Keys are interesting and attractive objects, as decorators have discovered. Ornate or plain, large or small, and of a great variety of materials, all keys have a mission — they move an obstacle or series of obstacles that prevents something from being opened. They are worth collecting in themselves; and are found in increasing numbers in antique shows and shops.

A word of caution: it seems that there are numbers of large wrought-iron keys now being made in Mexico, "aged" in lye, and sold to unsuspecting dealers and collectors as "Old Western Jail Keys." Had there been as many jails as there appear to be keys, it might almost seem there was one for everybody living west of the Mississippi before 1900! Bought cheaply, these keys are interesting, however, since most of them are handmade replicas of old Spanish and Mexican Colonial keys still to be found South of the Border. Some, of course, are genuine.

Since lockmakers are constantly improving both the precision and quality of their products (famous artists have been employed by Yale and Towne to design their hardware), a farsighted collector might do well to add some of these present day items to his collection. A recent news story told of a "great-grandmaster" key unlocking all 524 doors in the new Health, Education and Public Welfare Building in Richmond, Virginia. There were "grandmaster" keys for all the doors on any one floor; the most unusual of all was the key that worked on every lock while the building was under construction—but once any room had been unlocked with its regular key, this construction key would no longer work on the lock. Surely some lucky collector will eventually get this item!

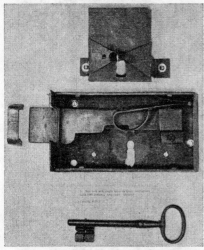

Late 18th cent. single lever tumbler.

Double-bitted key, with hollow shank holding second key, German, 17th cent.

Large key for spring mechanism lock, 17th century, German

Door Knockers and Porters

by CYRIL BRACEGIRDLE

I T WAS not until late in the 16th century that doors began to have knockers of any kind. The monasteries and cathedrals of the Middle Ages invariably carried on the main door a lion's head with a ring through its mouth. These were not true knockers, since there was no boss against which the ring could be struck; indeed, their principle use seems to have been to enable any wrong doer, fleeing from the soldiers or an enraged mob, to claim sanctuary by grasping the ring since they were then technically within the protection of the Church.

These rings were, however, the direct ancestors of the knocker. In the last decades of the 16th century, the blacksmiths of England began to make similar iron rings for the ordinary domestic door, and provided a metal plate on which the ring could be hammered. Sometimes the knocker took the shape of a mallet in imitation of the wooden mallet which Elizabethans often hung on a nail beside the door for visitors to knock with and make their presence known.

One of the earliest types of mass-produced knockers consisted of a simple iron piece swinging from pivots attached to a metal plate. These proved an incitement to young hooligans to test their muscles at the sport of knocker-wrenching. Sometimes after a night of revelry whole streets would awaken to find their knockers lying in the roadway. Largely because of this, the simple pivoted rapper went out of fashion.

More elaborate and secure knockers, made of cast instead of wrought iron, were developed. Animal head shapes became fashionable with the rapper swinging from mouth or nostrils.

There were rappers in the form of fruiting vines, or a hand grasping a

Spanish knocker in chiselled iron; late 16th century.

Victorian cast iron knockers from an illustrated catalog of hardware, ca. 1850.

bar. A classical vogue from the 1760s brought the vase shape, also Egyptian sphinx heads; and in 1839 the firm of Coalbrookdale, in the English county of Shropshire, introduced castings which could be hand-chased and highly burnished. A collector's item today is the knocker bearing a diamond-shaped mark which shows that the design was registered sometime between 1842 and 1883.

Along with knockers came the door porters, or door stops, most of which are of iron or brass and date from 1775 onwards. That was the year in which John Izon and Thomas Whitehurst of England patented their invention of the rising door hinge which caused a door to rise slightly as it opened and then to close again unless held—a boon even today, as any housewife with thick carpets will know.

The arrival on the domestic scene of the rising hinge undoubtedly helped to force the development of the door porter. Early examples were often in the shape of a basket of flowers, or a lion's paw. Often they were quite large and heavy. A crouching lion or sphinx could be up to 15 inches in height and weigh 3 to 5 pounds. Aristocrats had porters made in the form of their coat of arms.

In the mid-19th century, porters in imitation of celebrity figures appeared; there was the Duke of Wellington in a cocked hat. Admiral Nelson, and Queen Victoria in coronation robes. Punch and Judy shapes were popular,

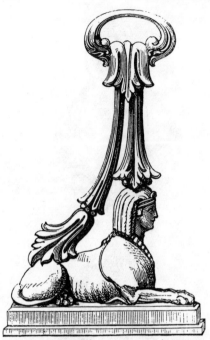

English cast-iron door porter; mid-Victorian period.

Cast-iron door porter- symbol of an "Englishman's Castle." Ca. 1870.

as also was a knight with sword and shield in symbolization of the guardian of the "Englishman's castle." The rarer items eagerly sought by collectors today are obelisks in Derbyshire marble. There are also domes in a clear green glass with elongated air bubbles trapped inside; these were made in Bristol and Nailsea.

Often the best sources from which to acquire knockers and porters are the sales of old houses, though the dusty recesses of English junk shops can also yield surprising treasures.

The invention of the electric bell effectively put an end to the manufacture of door knockers and porters.

Late Victorian door knockers; some, like the second trom the left in the top row, have the name of the resident engraved on a plain surface.

Paul Revere, Brass and Coppersmith

by CARL DREPPERD

MUCH has been written about Paul Revere, including Esther Forbes monumental "Paul Revere & The World He Lived In", published by Houghton Mifflin, 1942. This being the case, practically all articles and commentaries of the past decade have been so many twice-told tales, told all over again. New material on Paul Revere has indeed been scarce, but recently two happenings of importance make another essay on Paul Revere almost mandatory.

In 1788 Paul Revere acquired an iron furnace which he converted for the casting of bronze church bells and cannon. His first cast bronze bell was pulled from the sand of its mold and core in 1792. On that day Paul Revere entered a new business and became an active partner in the stabilization of our new nation. In 1794 he received an order to cast howitzers of 8.25 inch bore for the army. Our great wooden ship of the line, The Constitution, was then in process of building. The copper bolts required to build, and the copper to sheathe this frigate were ordered from England. Upon arrival, certain of the bolts were found to be of the wrong size. Revere remade them.

In 1800 he admitted that he had discovered the method of making copper malleable and rolling it hot. His first customer was the Commonwealth of Massachusetts, which purchased 7675 pounds of copper sheathing and 789 pounds of copper nails to cover the State House dome. The Commonwealth paid the bill quickly enough for Revere to meet his payrolls, while the Federal government lagged far behind and wondered whether it was necessary after all to give orders to our own productive facilities when it was so much easier for a bureaucrat simply to order the copper from England.

When Massachusetts paid Revere over $4000 for the copper for the State House dome he plowed the money back into copper production. His next job was to re-copper the Constitution and thus, for the first time, a U.S. ship was re-coppered with United States made sheeting.

In 1803 Revere did something that perhaps shocked the smart boys of the nation's capital. He told the Secretary of the Navy that he found it difficult to procure stocks of new or old copper, that merchants were not in the habit of importing it. He therefore suggested that the ships of the U.S. Navy purchase copper at Smyrna and bring home a number

Paul Revere & Son,

At their BELL *and* CANNON FOUNDERY, *at the*
North Part of BOSTON,

CAST BELLS, of all fizes ; every kind of Brafs ORDNANCE, and every kind of *Compofition Work*, for SHIPS, &c. *at the fhorteft notice ;* Manufacture COPPER into SHEETS, BOLTS. SPIKES, NAILS, RIVETS, DOVETAILS, &c. from *Malleable Copper.*

They always keep, by them, every kind of *Copper foftening for Ships.* They have now on hand, a number of Church and Ship Bells, of different fizes ; a large quantity of Sheathing Copper, from 16 up to 30 ounce ; Bolts, Spikes, Nails, &c of all fizes, which they warrant equal to Englifh manufacture.

Cafh and the higheft price given for old Copper and Brafs ·

march 10

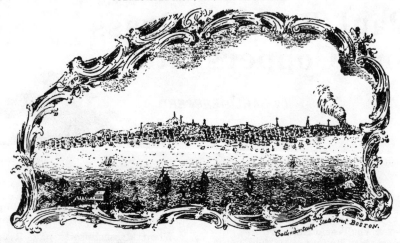

Early View of Boston. That dense smoke on the horizon is from Paul Revere's Foundry. The date of this print is 1788. It is views of this kind that make collecting Industrial and Commercial Americana a most interesting pursuit.

of tons. The first U.S. vessel to do this was the Constitution. The copper business was launched.

In 1804 Joseph Warren Revere, son of Paul, was made a partner in the business and given a one-third interest in his father's property, then valued at $16,200. In this deed Paul Revere, the father, is listed as a "gentleman", and his son Joseph Warren as a bell and cannon founder. Paul Revere continued as a gentleman should who still owned a two-thirds interest in a business. He acted as chairman of the board, so to speak, and sent his son abroad on a fact-finding visit to the copper-making countries of Europe—England, Wales, France and Scandinavia. In 1805 Joseph Warren returned to continue the expansion of the infant industry founded by night rider Paul Revere.

The business, if it didn't boom, certainly made excellent progress. Off its rollers came copper to roof public buildings and private dwellings, and stock for the merchants of Canada, the New England states, and the Atlantic seaboard. Coppersmiths were calling on Revere for sheet copper and technical advice. Robert Fulton wrote to Revere in 1808: "I am informed you have a mill for roleing of copper and that you furnish it in any size. I wish to have

a quantity of 12 pound to the square foot and should be glad to know your price and when it could be delivered." This was copper for the boiler of the world's first truly successful steamboat, the Clermont. From then on Fulton turned to Revere for the boiler copper of his every new steamboat and the records of the company indicate business to the volume of over $10,000.

Revere, of course, was being undersold by the British copper producers and, in Revere's opinion, imports were encouraged by our Treasury's laxity of tariff provision. Revere spoke for a 17½% duty on all copper except pigs and bars, and said that plate should be included as manufactured copper. Because of a twisted interpretation of the law, he had to pay full tariff on scrap copper sheathing that had been taken from ships in foreign docks!

Thus began an industry which, by the time of the War of 1812, found the U.S. Navy ready for action because we had copper for ship bottoms and bronze for guns.

Perhaps, from a collecting standpoint, nothing more need be said except that every collector should do his best to procure a copy of "Paul Revere—Pioneer Industrialist" and read the story from cover to cover. This is a booklet the like of which should be published by every company in America. If there be any who say they are so late in point of time that they have no antiquarian background, let them hide their heads in shame. Every business in America has an antiquarian background, either objectively or subjectively. When that background is brought to light it exposes facts which make the history of business a revelation and not a lot of mumbo-jumbo.

Early American Brass and Copper... and its makers

by HENRY J. KAUFFMAN

Typical Pennsylvania teakettle, signed by W. Heiss, 123 North Third St. Philadelphia, in rare 6½" diameter size. Most are 8 to 10" in diameter; a few are 12".

THE QUANTITIES OF copper and brass wares found in antiques shops in this country focus attention on the fact that though pieces may look alike they are not always equal in value. All copper teakettles, for example, appear essentially the same wherever they were made. While there is little difference in the value of imported English and Scandinavian kettles, the average American copper teakettle is worth a great deal more than either. This conclusion applies in a general way to all antiques, but it is recognized more acutely in the field of copper and brass because of the difficulty in determining the place of origin.

The historical perspective of coppersmithing in America might start as early as 1738 when Peacock Rigger advertised in the *Pennsylvania Gazette* that he was located in Philadelphia, "in Market Street, near the Sign of the Indian King," where he made and sold all kinds of copper work.

In the *Pennsylvania Journal* of September 4, 1766, Benjamin Harbeson announced he had removed his shop to the corner of Laetitia Court. He listed himself ready to serve on reasonable terms in such copper work as "stills, brewing coppers, sugar boilers, copper fish kettles, teakettles, boilers, soap coppers, brass and copper washing kettles, stew pans, frying pans, capuchin plate warmers, brass and copper scales, warming pans, chafing dishes, chocolate pots, copper ships' stoves, silversmith's boilers, brass and iron candlesticks, brass cocks of all sorts," and various items of London pewter, bell metal, and tin.

This imposing list of objects made by one man before the American Revolution indicates that there was a sizeable production of these objects at that time. Not all coppersmiths who worked at the trade until about 1850 made as wide a range of objects as Mr. Harbeson. However, styles changed very little as long as these objects were made by hand. The function of stills, for example, changed little throughout the period; hence the shapes remained much the same. The same is true of skillets, stewpans, warming pans, and the like.

It is important to note that many of

the objects named in early advertisements in America have never been found or identified with a maker. The writer has never seen, definitely attributed to an American maker, brewing coppers, sugar boilers, soap boilers, washing coppers, copper ships' stoves and other of the items enumerated. Objects he has seen that have been positively identified as American products include one or two each of warming pans, liquid measures, stew pans, skillets, half-bushel measures, many copper kettles, and hundreds of copper teakettles.

A number of large copper kettles for making apple butter were made by the Schaum family in Lancaster, Pennsylvania. However, this particular use has never been found listed among products made by an 18th or early 19th century coppersmith. Kettles for making apple butter were not lined with tin as most other vessels were. Schaum kettles, made until 1926, were widely distributed through the country by Sears, Roebuck & Company.

The scarcity of stills, signed or un-

Copper frying pan made in Philadelphia, though maker's name cannot be distinguished. Possibly made by Bentley, a Philadelphia craftsman who made interesting forms and signed many pieces.

Copper measure by Holmes & Evans, Fisherville, N. H. Measures of copper are common, but signed ones are very rare. The sets were used for selling liquor to the retail trade at distilleries.

Unusually attractive brass warming pan with maker's intaglio stamp under group of holes near top showing initial "C" and a possible, though indistinct "A P." Surprisingly few warming pans, either of brass or copper, were signed, though almost every coppersmith of the 18th century mentioned them in his advertising. It is Mr. Kauffman's opinion that those which do exist with name of craftsman engraved on the lids are imported. Of the 3 marked pans in his own collection, none can positively be attributed to an American craftsman. One has an intaglio stamp with initials "I W" on the hinge, which might be interpreted as Joshua Witherle, a coppersmith in Boston in 1789. However, attribution of this type is precarious.

FRANCIS SANDERSON,
COPPERSMITH from LANCASTER, living in
GAY-STREET, BALTIMORE-TOWN, a few
Doors above Mr. *Andrew Steiger's,*

MAKES and fells all forts of COPPER-WORK,
viz. ftills of all fizes, fifh and wafh kettles,
copper and brafs, brewing-kettles, faucepans, coffee
and chocolate pots, ftew-pans, and Dutch ovens. He
fells any of the above articles as cheap as can be imported from *England,* and carries on his Bufinefs in
Lancafter as ufual. He likewife carries on the TIN-
BUSINESS in all its branches. Country fhop-keepers
may be fupplied, either by wholefale or retail, and all
others fent from the country fhall be carefully executed.

Advertisement from the *Maryland Journal and Baltimore Ad-
vertiser,* August 20, 1773. Sanderson worked in Lancaster, Pa.
before the Revolution, later in Baltimore. At least one signed
piece is known; others may exist in the Pennsylvania-Maryland
region.

signed, is curious, considering how many were made and how widely they were used. Of the half dozen the writer has seen, only three were marked.

It must be obvious to the reader that this perspective on early coppersmithing is focusing directly toward Pennsylvania. Though coppersmiths were working all over the Colonies, more signed pieces have been found by Pennsylvania craftsmen than the rest of the country put together. It may be that more Pennsylvania craftsmen signed their products, but it is the writer's opinion that the bulk of 18th century coppersmithing, and a great deal in the 19th century, was done in the Keystone State. A small number of New York coppersmiths signed their work, and there are scattered examples from New England and the South, but the main route for signed pieces seems to be from Philadelphia to Pittsburgh. Perhaps John Getz of Lancaster signed more pieces of copper ware than any other American coppersmith.

In identifying objects of copper and brass, a connoisseur may know styles well enough to attribute unmarked objects to American craftsmen or to European sources. For instance, teakettles with a hinged lid on the spout are regarded as foreign; no American examples are known. This need not mean that one signed by an American craftsman

may not be found tomorrow. Such an exception will not greatly change the conclusion, for principles are not established on one or two exceptions.

The only sure method of identifying an American object of copper or brass is by finding a *bona fide* name of an American craftsman on it. A name alone is not proof of American production as a number of European craftsmen placed their names on their products. In the columns below are listed some of the craftsmen known to have worked in sheet copper and brass in America, with an identifying date. Any of their names *might* be found on an early brass or copper piece.

John Morrison's mark on handle of copper teakettle is a rare impression; hardness of copper and large size of stamps produced few such nearly perfect impressions.

Some American Coppersmiths
from Contemporary Records

Apple, Jacob	Philadelphia	1852
Apple, Philip	Philadelphia	1811
Attlee, William	Lancaster, Pa.	1790
Babb, John	Reading, Pa.	1806
Babb, Mathias	Reading, Pa.	1796
Bailey, William	Maryland & Pa.	1770 -1800
Beader, Henry	Harrisburg, Pa.	1820 -1826
Benson, John	New York	1841
Bentley, David	Philadelphia	1842 -1852
Bigger, Peacock	Philadelphia and Annapolis	1740 -1750
Bintzel, Daniel	Philadelphia	1842
Bintzel, William	Philadelphia	1852
Blanc, Victor	Philadelphia	1811
Bratzman, Andreas	Reading, Pa.	1813
Brotherton, E.	Lancaster, Pa.	1806
Brown, Thomas	Philadelphia	1852
Bruce, John	Baltimore	1850
Buchanan, James	Pittsburgh	1818
Buckhard, Peter	New York	1841
Carpenter, Alfred	Boston	1848
Carter, John	Boston	1848
Chessen, George	Philadelphia	1811
Clark, Forbes	Harrisburg, Pa.	1814
Clemm & Bailey	Baltimore	1784
Coltman, J. W.	Boston	1848
Cook, John	Philadelphia	1811
Cropley, John	Philadelphia	1852
Cunningham, Wm.	New York	1841
Darby, William	New York	1841
Davis & Wiley	Pittsburgh	1837
Deich, John	Philadelphia	1840
Delaney, John	Carlisle, Pa.	1792
Dickey, Isaiah & Co.	Pittsburgh Maryland & Pa.	1837 1770 -1800
Diller, Samuel	Lancaster, Pa.	1869
Dusenbury, Thomas	New York	1841
Dverter, Wm.	Lancaster, Pa.	1869
Eicholtz, Jacob	Lancaster, Pa.	1810
Eisenhut, John	Philadelphia	1811
Eisenhut, John D.	Philadelphia	1852
Fisher, Charles	York, Pa.	1832
Foos, Jacob	Lancaster, Pa.	1869
Forrest, Jacob	Lancaster, Pa.	1869
Gallagher, P.	Boston	1848
Getz, John	Lancaster, Pa.	1817 -1835
Gould, Joseph	Boston	1848
Graff, Joseph	Philadelphia	1852
Grauel, Daniel	Philadelphia	1811
Grimes, James	Pittsburgh	1837
Haldane, James	Philadelphia	1765
Hammett & Hiles	Philadelphia	1840
Hannah & Launy	New York	1841
Harberger, Henry	Philadelphia	1811
Harbeson, Benjamin	Philadelphia	1790
Harbeson, Joseph	Philadelphia	1766
Harbeson, Joseph	Pittsburgh	1807
Harley, Francis	Philadelphia	1840
Hasler, John	New York	1841
Heiss, Goddard	Philadelphia	1852
Heiss, Wm. Jr.	Philadelphia	1852
Heller, Henry	Philadelphia	1840
Hemmenway, B.	Boston	1848
Hill and Chamberlin	Boston	1848
Howard & Rodgers	Pittsburgh	1837
Hunneman & Co.	Boston	1848
Hutton, William	Philadelphia	1840
Jewell, Charles	New York	1841
Keefer, J & F.	Pittsburgh	1837
Kidd, John	Reading, Pa.	1790 -1800
Knox, Edward	New York	1841
Kower, John	Kutztown, Pa.	1841
Leacock, William	Philadelphia	1840
Lee, William	Philadelphia	1852
LeFrentz, George	York, Pa.	1783
Lightbody, Collin	New York	1841
Lindsay, David	Carlisle, Pa.	1792
Lock & Cordwell	Boston	1848
Loring, A. B.	Boston	1848
Loring, John G.	Boston	1848
Lyne, John	Harrisburg, Pa.	1811
Lyne, Robert	Philadelphia	1800
McBride, John	York, Co. Pa.	1783
McCauley, John	Philadelphia	1800
McCoy, Neil	York, Pa.	1784
Megee, George	Philadelphia	1840 -1852
Meredith, John	Philadelphia	1840
Miller, F.	Chambersburg, Pa.	1800
Miller, Jacob	Harrisburg, Pa.	1820
Minshall, Thomas	Middletown, Pa.	1802
Morrison, John	Philadelphia	1790
Noble, James	Philadelphia	1840
Oat, George	Philadelphia	1852
Oat, Israel	Philadelphia	1852
Oat, Jesse	Philadelphia	1811
Oat, Joseph	Philadelphia	1840
Oat, Joseph & Son	Philadelphia	1852
O'Bryon, Benjamin	Philadelphia	1840
Orr, Robert	Philadelphia	1800
Peters & Co.	Philadelphia	1811
Pier, Benjamin	New York	1841
Potter, James	Philadelphia	1790
Raborg, Christopher	Baltimore	1785
Read, W.	Philadelphia	1840
Reed, Robert	Lancaster, Pa.	1795
Reigart, Henry	Lancaster, Pa.	1803
Rink, Miller H.	Philadelphia	1840
Roberts & Son	Philadelphia	1840
Roberts, Israel	Philadelphia	1811 -1852
Roberts, James	Philadelphia	1852
Rulon, Jane	Philadelphia	1852
Schaum, Benjamin	Lancaster, Pa.	1790
Schaum, Peter	Lancaster, Pa.	1790
Schoenfelder	Reading, Pa.	1803
Seffron, George	York, Pa.	1789
Shenfelder, Asop	Reading, Pa.	1838
Shuler, George	Middletown, Pa.	1803
Simons, John	Philadelphia	1852
Stafford, Spencer	Albany, N. Y.	1794
Steele, George	Hartford, Conn.	1790
Stoehr, Daniel	Hanover, Pa.	1787 -1863
Strickler, Issac	Philadelphia	1811
Sweet, William	New York	1841
Thayer, Cornelius	Litchfield	1785
Thompson, John	Harrisburg, Pa.	1814
Tophan, Reuben	Philadelphia	1800
Town, John	Pittsburgh	1813
Trueman, Thomas	Philadelphia	1790
Tryon, George	Philadelphia	1811
Upperman, John	Lancaster, Pa.	1811
Varley, Abram	Marietta, Pa.	1814
Waters & Milk	Boston	1848
Weitzel, George	Lancaster, Pa.	1830
West, Jacob	Philadelphia	1840
Whitaker, Robert	Philadelphia	1811
Williamson, Isaac	New York	1841
Winter, Jonathan	York Co. Pa.	1788
Witherle, Joshua & Co.	Boston	1789
Witman, John	Kutztown, Pa.	1804
Wright, John	New York	1841
Yeates, Edmund	Philadelphia	1811
Youse, George	Harrisburg, Pa.	1807 -1814

Ornate brass wall sconces and standing pulpit lights for one or two candles. These ranged in price from 6 to 12 schillings each.

Old English Brasses of the Late Georgian Period

by BENJAMIN EDWARDS

Clock brasses, capitals, bases, etc., for wooden columns.

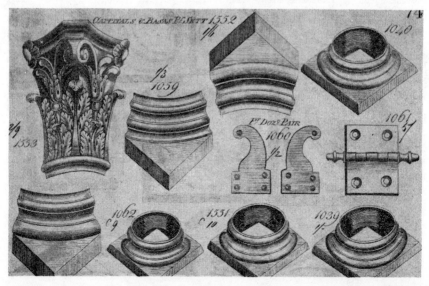

WHAT is a "rapper?" "Rapper," in the England of 1825 meant what we call a knocker; a door knocker. In case anyone wonders, whether or not these items entered our country from England as early to mid 19th century imports, the answer is yes, and in great quantities. In fact they have never ceased to enter. From at least 1900, they have entered as reproductions, made by reputable old firms. Perhaps reproduction is not the correct term. Certainly, in some cases, brass items have been made in the same way, from the same pattern, for a century and a half, by the same firm. Therefore the proper term would be continuous production and not reproduction. Furthermore, a surprising number of rappers and other brasses are now entering the country as antiques—for they date prior to 1830.

Fully to understand this brass situation it is necessary to know that Birmingham, England, has been a brass and cutlery city for lo, these many scores of years, adding up to three or more centuries. Birmingham brass barrels for pistols and guns have been imported since, it is said, 1700. There are other experts who insist that Eltweed Pomeroy, the early gunsmith of the Pilgrim Company made pistols with barrels of "Brummagem Brass".

The fact of early or late making of brass items in traditional forms, and of modern castings from ancient patterns, cannot be determined by textual demonstrations. One must know brass, patterns and sources. Late productions, shipped here as new goods, will have country of origin marking . . . or should have. But old items are now coming in as imports sponsored by a small army of keen dealers who tour England and the Continent at some profit, just buying glass, china, and brass items of antiquity for resale.

The illustrations selected for this text are direct from the original catalog of a Union of Birmingham brass founders who sold goods for domestic use and for export. You will find their

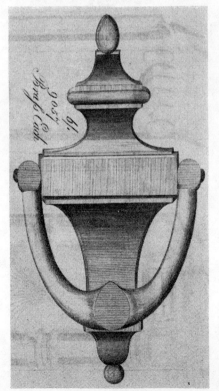 

So-called Colonial rapper, actually of the Adam period, and hand and shell rapper.

clock balls, capitals, bases, and hinges on many American clocks. Similarly, you will find "rappers" on many old American homes, and the sconces and lighting fixtures still used in untouched early homes and properly in certain restorations.

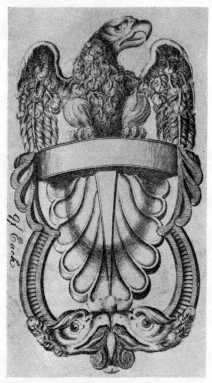

Eagle brass door rapper which cost 9 schillings in 1825. In bronze or cast iron the price was 3 schillings.

No. 1

No. 2

Brass Trivets—
The Old and
the New

by WILLIAM PALEY

Back of No. 1

No. 3

IS IT POSSIBLE to distinguish between old trivets and modern reproductions? Many collectors of old
trivets are frustrated by the difficulty
experienced in doing so; others simply
avoid collecting brass trivets entirely,
realizing that it is so easy to "age" a
modern one.

In response to several recent re-
quests for help, here are a few guides:
1. On the authentic old brass and
copper trivets, since the work was
hand-done, the legs almost invariably
pierce the tops. (No's. 1, 2, 6, 7, 9, 10,
11, 12, and 13.) The top will be of
sheet metal of uniform thickness
which may be from 1/16 to 3/16
inches. Cast brass trivets are not
common, but when found, the legs
are cast integral with the top (No.
14).

2. The top of an old trivet is quite
often warped and uneven as a result
of holding heavy objects, of being
used as a stepping stool, and of being
dropped, thus bending the point. (No.
12, and No. 13 detail.)

3. The uniform application of bangs
and nicks is suspect. There are certain places where a trivet will usually
get marked, depending on the type of
use it has had. (See No. 7) I have one
trivet which was obviously used as a
hammer to drive a nail. One edge is
badly scarred; otherwise it is unmarked.

4. The upper surface of the trivet
will be much smoother than the un-
derside. (No. 1 detail.) The smoothing effort was concentrated on the

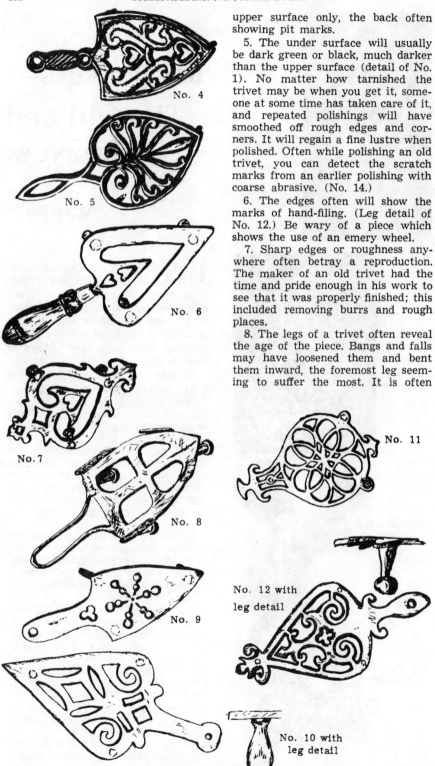

No. 4

No. 5

No. 6

No. 7

No. 8

No. 9

No. 11

No. 12 with
leg detail

No. 10 with
leg detail

upper surface only, the back often showing pit marks.

5. The under surface will usually be dark green or black, much darker than the upper surface (detail of No. 1). No matter how tarnished the trivet may be when you get it, someone at some time has taken care of it, and repeated polishings will have smoothed off rough edges and corners. It will regain a fine lustre when polished. Often while polishing an old trivet, you can detect the scratch marks from an earlier polishing with coarse abrasive. (No. 14.)

6. The edges often will show the marks of hand-filing. (Leg detail of No. 12.) Be wary of a piece which shows the use of an emery wheel.

7. Sharp edges or roughness anywhere often betray a reproduction. The maker of an old trivet had the time and pride enough in his work to see that it was properly finished; this included removing burrs and rough places.

8. The legs of a trivet often reveal the age of the piece. Bangs and falls may have loosened them and bent them inward, the foremost leg seeming to suffer the most. It is often

more bent; its forward edge is more worn and rounded. (Detail of No. 1.) The same applies to the outer edges of the other two legs. Uniform rounding of all edges of all legs is suspect.

9. Become familiar with the patterns being reproduced, and the characteristics of these trivets, their size and weight, type and length of leg, where and how they have been marked by their maker, since honorable makers of reproductions will stamp their product. Be suspicious of seeing several brass trivets of the same or varying design, all with identical aging characteristics, at the same time, in the same place. Old brass trivets are not likely to be found that way.

10. No single one of the above points, but a combination of all of them is the best way to identify an old trivet. Sometimes, even with all of these in mind, you cannot be sure. Some dealers, unfortunately, give trivets a bath which removes all dirt and aging from front and back.

No. 14

KEY TO ILLUSTRATIONS

No's. 3, 4, 5; Three of the most commonly reproduced designs in brass as well as in iron.

No. 6: A wooden handle is almost a sure indication of an old trivet. The rosewood handle and brass ferrule make this brass heart trivet distinctive.

No. 7: The three legs which had worked themselves loose were ineptly tightened by hammering the trivet surface leaving dents.

No. 8: A rather clumsy, hand-made brass stand with handle, legs, and lugs brazed to the heavy sheet metal body, and the entire trivet coarsely hand filed.

Brass trivets with dowel-type iron legs, such as *No. 9,* or turned iron legs, like *No. 10,* that pierce the surface are old. Most brass trivets have brass legs. The pendulum-style trivet *(No. 11)* has three mismatched legs; quite often a loose leg was lost, and a substitute was added.

No's. 12, 13, 14: A popular design was often copied by different craftsmen, leading to slight variations. The hole in the handles of *No's. 12 and 14* are later improvements on the earlier *No. 13.* The earliest of the three, *No. 13,* is of thinner brass than some trivets and hence, as the side view shows, has been bent out of shape. *No. 14* is of cast brass with integral legs and body.

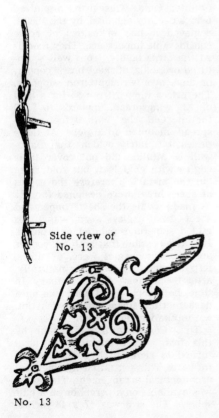

Side view of
No. 13

No. 13

Eagles of Brass, Copper and Zinc

*The Centennial Eagle of Bakewell &
Mullins, made at the Salem, Ohio factory
of this firm. It is the same type of eagle
that decorated the parapets of Centennial
Buildings, 1876.*

by CHARLES MULLINS

MANUFACTURED BY BAKEWELL & MULLINS, SALEM, OHIO

EAGLE COLLECTING is no longer a limited cult. Neither is it a vogue. It is a growing pursuit which no longer draws the line at carved wood eagles by the mass producer, Bellamy or the itinerant ne'er-do-well Schimmel. Now our eagle collectors seek any and all eagle forms, whether weather vanes, architectural decoration, ship figure heads, overdoor or hatchway pieces, or just room decoration. The collectors cannot, somehow, concern themselves over and seek for rarities in Eagles such as the magnificent examples carved by Dr. Grier, by Benjamin Rush or Samuel Skillin. Instead they must, to be successful collectors—and a successful collector, some believe, is one who achieves possession of the object of his quest—find eagles that were made in sufficient quantities so as to survive in great enough numbers to be found.

One important such a source of eagle manufacture was the Architectural Ornament Works of Bakewell & Mullins, at Salem, Columbiana County, Ohio. This firm, organized over a century ago, had, by the 1880's, achieved a line of eagles of some considerable importance. They modeled the birds boldly, from well sculptured originals, of sheet brass, copper, or zinc, over wrought iron supports. The prices ranged from $5 for a bird of 12″ wingspread, upwards to $210 for an "Old Abe" with 9 foot wingspread, mounted on a globe. At these prices it is fairly evident that Bakewell & Mullins did not cover their eagles with gold leaf, but sold them "in the metal". Therefore the eagles of sheet brass were designed for use as made, while the sheet copper and sheet zinc eagles were sometimes gilded, sometimes painted, or bronzed. It is also possible that both the copper and the zinc eagles were, at times, left unpainted, to weather naturally, after the manner of lead statuary. In time, both copper and zinc take on a dark mottled surface of greyish tint, not unlike weathered stone.

The "Centennial Eagle" made by this firm was available with head turned to right, to left, or straightforward. This permitted symmetrical architectural arrangement. This eagle was available on a perch, or on a half sphere. The size was 47 x 48 inches.

On perch, the price was $30; on half sphere, $32.

The "Trade" eagle, with 6 foot wingspread was probably designated as trade type because it was designed for use as a sign. It should be remembered that "Eagle" was a favorite business name. Many towns had an eagle works of some sort or other. Some had an Eagle brewery, some an Eagle chair factory, Eagle soap works, Eagle pharmacy, Eagle mirror works, Eagle pottery and so on.

The firm also made a gigantic Mural Eagle with 14 foot wingspread. This was an eagle in low relief, wings outspread, head thrust through a 13 starred wreath, one talon supporting the U. S. Shield, the other grasping arrows and ribbons. When tightly affixed to a wall, this eagle could be treated as a carving, or pargetry decoration; it was, however equally applicable to an exterior wall, especially within the confines of a gable, or similar architectural area. The price of this grand eagle was $200.

Bakewell & Mullins made "Old Abe" the major eagle of their collection. This bird, with 9 foot wingspread, was available on the type of base shown (actually the upper area of the field of a shield), or mounted on a half sphere. Old Abe is depicted in his most famous pose, that of the living standard carried by Wisconsin troops in the War-between-the-States. This

Top, "Old Abe"; center, "Trade Eagle" and bottom, the Mural Eagle for interior or exterior walls. All illustrations from original art supplied by the manufacturers, and used in the 1880's.

is not a fairy tale. Old Abe was a live eagle, trained to sit on a perch carried in a parade. When the Wisconsin boys were mustered in the Union Army, Old Abe was taken along and carried as a living standard in battle. He became a very famous bird indeed; was exhibited at the Centennial and has had a place in the Wisconsin State Capitol building. The price of this Old Abe was $200 perched on the shield top, and $210 perched on a half-sphere.

Weather Vanes

by ALBERT CHRISTIAN REVI

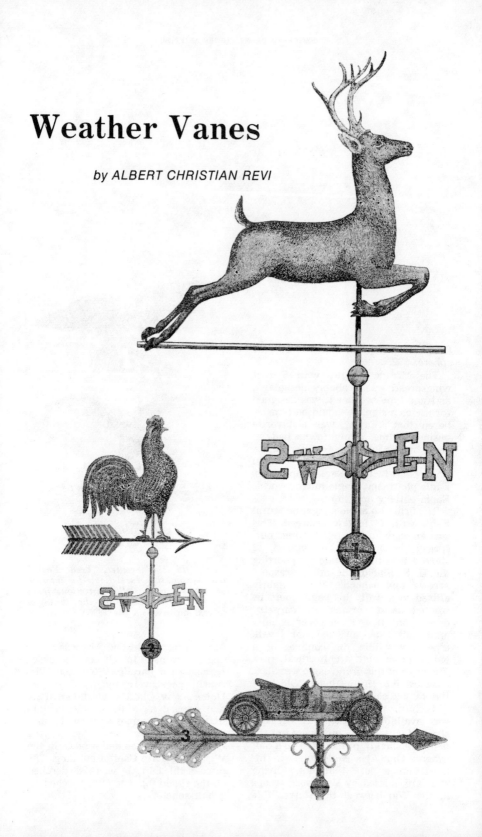

EVER since they were elevated to the classification of "Folk Art" and "Primitives," early handmade weather vanes have become too difficult, and too expensive, for collectors of modest means to acquire. As a result, many people have begun to collect weather vanes produced after 1850, using them for decorative purposes inside and outside the home.

About 1928, E. G. Washburne & Company, at that time located at 207 Fulton Street, Brooklyn, New York, published a catalog of their weather vanes. Some of the designs shown had been carried over a period of several years, but the catalog indicated that new designs—like the car weather vanes—were in the offing at all times. Illustrations of gilded, full-bodied and swell-bodied animals—cows, bulls, deer, dogs, horses, roosters, sheep, hogs, eagles, and fish—predominated, but there were also designs featuring sloops and schooners, windmills, and a quill pen. Silhouette weather vanes made of flat copper, finished in gold leaf or statuary bronze, or any special color, were shown on the last few pages of the catalog.

The E. G. Washburne Company was established in 1853, and un-

1. Gilded deer; swell-bodied and full-bodied models in 20" and 30" lengths. 2. Swell-bodied roosters of gilded copper were produced in various sizes—14", 18", 24" and 28". 3. Gilded, swell-bodied runabout mounted on arrow 26" long. 4. Windmill, 18" high, rod with fence and dog, 42" long, were made of copper finished in gold leaf, statuary bronze, or any special color. 5. Cardinal point designs identified with commercial manufacturers of weather vanes. Top to bottom: L. W. Cushing, J. W. Fiske, W. A. Snow, E. G. Washburne, R. Watkins, and two unknown manufacturers whose vanes are often seen. (Illustration from **Weathervanes and Whirligigs**, by Ken Fitzgerald.) 6. Full-bodied sloops and schooners of gilded copper, 36" and 48" long. 7. Gilded quill pen weather vanes ranged in size from 1 ½ to 6 ft. long. 8. Flying ducks, in silhouette, 30" long. 9. Silhouette of milkmaid and cow, 30" and 47" in length.

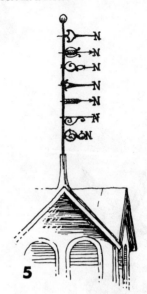

5

doubtedly they manufactured many unusual weather vanes, both before and after their 1928 catalog was printed. The firm was listed as the Washburne Weather Vane Company in the 1965 edition of the New York City Directory, but no mention of it was found in subsequent editions. Ken Fitzgerald's new book, *Weathervanes and Whirligigs* (Clarkson N. Potter, Inc., Publishers), gives Washburne's present address as 85 Andover Street, Boston, Mass., and advises that new "old" weather vanes can be purchased from the company, or from one of their distributors.

Tin Cookie Cutters, Molds, and Sconces

by ALICE WILT STRAUSS

One of a pair of early tin sconces with high narrow back bent forward to form hood. Author's collection.

FOR many weeks before Christmas the Pennsylvania Dutch housewife was busy making preparations for the holiday season, for the festivities did not end on December 26, but were carried over into the weeks that followed. She had to be well supplied for her holiday entertaining. There had to be cookies for the friends who came "putzing," and cookies and coffee and home-made wine to serve to the men who came on New Year's Day to "shoot in the New Year." The Christmas cookie was as traditional with the Pennsylvania Dutch as the Putz or the tree.

Only at this particular time of the year did the "fancy" cutters come into use, and from the rolled dough came stars and angels, household and farm animals, birds and flowers. Some of these cookie figures took their places on the tree with the candy canes and popcorn strings, but most of them were used for the holiday entertaining.

Many of these "fancy" cutters are still to be found, some in fine condition, and collectors are gathering them up to use, or simply to add to their collection of primitives, as examples of a type of life which is fading into history. But the tradition of the Christmas cookie is still observed in many sections of the Dutchland.

Conflicting stories have been told regarding the inspiration for the designs on these cutters, so without proper authentication it would be difficult to state defini-

tely what prompted the choice of patterns. Some folks say the star, the angel, the camel, sheep, etc., were inspired by the figures of the nativity, and the Germans' love of the Putz. But other designs not associated with the Christmas characters are found as frequently as those mentioned. These must have had their origin elsewhere.

The horse was a favorite subject and is found in standing or running position. The pig, sheep, goat, donkey, cat, and the dog in a variety of breeds, would indicate that the tinsmith derived many of his ideas from the farm. He used also the rooster, the hen, the duck, and birds which are not easily recognized.

The eagle, which is a favorite Pennsylvania Dutch pattern, is considered one of the most desirable by collectors. But the tinsmith must have looked to other sources as well, for the forest animals have turned up on the cutters—bears, lions, foxes and others. The deer, though not as common as the barnyard animals or some of the others, is found often enough to make the search for the unusual worthwhile.

It has been suggested that these out-of-the-ordinary cutters were a necessary in-

Rare cookie mold about 20″ square; pudding mold; cheese mold. Owned by Ruth Briggs, Rockford, Ill.

vention of the tinsmith when he found his customer already well-supplied with cutters in the conventional patterns. In the very early days the housewife's only opportunity to obtain her tinware was through the visit of the itinerant tinsmith. Traveling from farm to farm, the tinsmith would produce, on the spot, the items needed by each family. Perhaps the housewife had her own ideas about the designs she wished on her cutters. Or perhaps, as was suggested, she was well supplied with the usual array and wanted something unusual.

Most of the cutters were small, the largest being, perhaps, not more than six or seven inches long, although pictured with the pudding mold, is a rare cutter measuring about twenty inches square. The figure is a rabbit. The earliest cutters were without handles, but most of them had "air holes."

Some of the patterns had two sets of cutting edges. The outside edge cut through the dough, while the other cutting edge was not as deep and served to make an impression on the surface of the cookie. Thus instead of the cookie being merely a figure in outline, interest was heightened by the addition of features on a man or woman, for instance, and by the details of the clothing. Some of the figures most eagerly sought by the collectors are the Colonial horseback rider, the Revolutionary soldier, the Indians, men or women; Uncle Sam, Mennonite figures and other historical figures representative of the progress of the period.

But the cookie cutters were not the only collectible examples of the tinsmith's art.

Collection of cookie cutters showing: horse standing and running, deer, dogs, lion, pig, eagle, 2 other birds. Owned by Ruth Briggs, Rockford, Ill.

There were the tin coffee pots of the early nineteenth century, the only decoration being the design in punched tin. Unlike the designs of the punched tin food safes, those on the coffee pots were not punched through. The pattern showed up in a series of raised dots on the surface of the pot, and it was applied to the tin before the tin was shaped.

The tin pudding molds and cheese molds could be as useful today as they were in the nineteenth century. A good boiling to assure cleanliness, perhaps a bit of solder on loose joints, and the mold would be as good as new. A punched tin lantern might add a decorative note to a home furnished in Early American, but its usefulness for lighting should not be depended upon. However, there are many tin candlesticks which could be useful, and some of the wall sconces. These sconces were made in several different styles and frequently can be found in shops, though pairs are getting pretty scarce.

Most decorative of these were the mirror sconces. These consisted of a round tin plate, slightly concave, which was covered with small mirrors set in "S" circular pattern. This plate hung against the wall, and a bracket at the base held the candle or candles. The mirrors, reflecting the light, produced a pleasing effect and also increased the efficiency of the fixture for illumination. Another type of wall sconce was similar to the one described above but was without the mirrors. This had a round tin plate, much like a pie tin, which hung against the wall, and was usually plain except for a fluted edge. The candle bracket extended from the base. Still another type had a high narrow back bent forward to form a hood. This hood was usually fluted.

Not infrequently the itinerant tinsmith was called upon to produce a particular piece to suit the whimsy of a housewife—a small box for trinkets, a decorative mirror frame, or even a toy or two. Exhibited at a show a few years ago was a doll house which had been brought from the Pennsylvania Dutch country. The exhibitor explained the house had been made on order by an itinerant tinsmith, and it is fun to let one's imagination roam a bit and picture the delight of some little girl years ago, when she awoke on Christmas morning to find the beloved Putz, and the pretty tin doll house beneath her tree.

Tin Candlemolds

by DONALD R. and CAROL M. RAYCRAFT

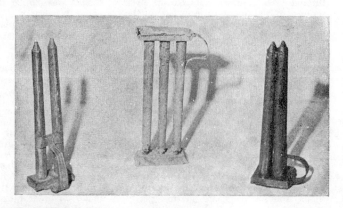

Above: Tin molds with 2, 3 or 4 tubes were used by American housewives in the early 19th century. Below: A rare 12 tube copper candlemold; early 19th century. Tin candlemold with an unusual arrangement
of its 6 tubes; early 19th century. Authors' collection.

IN HIS definitive study on early lighting devices, Arthur Hayward (3) comments, "candlemolds a few years ago were very plentiful and lightly valued, but the demands of collectors have become so insistent lately as to practically sweep the market here."

Mr. Hayward's statement is familiar to collectors of early lighting, primitives, and country antiques and accessories. The difficulty in acquiring candlemolds is further emphasized when one considers that Hayward's comment was made over 40 years ago. His book, *Colonial Lighting,* was first published in 1923 and a second edition was issued in 1927.

Erwin Christensen (1) writes that "candlemolds tell at a glance how candles were made. It (the candlemold) is purely utilitarian yet extremely attractive." Candlemolds vary greatly in size and shape, ranging from single tube molds to molds containing as many as nine dozen or more tubes. The most common candlemolds contain 4, 6, 8, or 12 tubes. Candlemolds are usually constructed of tin. However, early pine framed pewter molds containing from two to three dozen tubes are available. Candlemolds made of copper are scarce, though much later than the framed pewter molds.

Among the most sought after candlemolds are molds with an odd number of tubes or those with an unusual arrangement of tubes within the mold. Most candlemolds are rectangular in shape. Among collectors the most sought after mold is the rare round candlemold. This mold has the tubes within it arranged in a circular fashion rather than in a rectangular or square pattern. The authors recently witnessed a round 12-tube mold sell for $180 at an auction.

Candles were considered a great luxury in colonial America. A prime request when the colonies were being supplied with British goods was for tallow and candles. The major difficulty in making candles in colonial America was finding a substitute for beef tallow. Cattle were not plentiful in the colonies until the late seventeenth century. Among the several substitutes for the scarce tallow were wax from the honey combs of wild bees and spermaceti.

Spermaceti is a waxy substance obtained from the head of the sperm whale. It was found in a thick, oily form. Whale fat and blubber also

were a source for spermaceti. The spermaceti emerges as a mass of flaky white crystals. As much as 12 to 15 pounds of spermaceti could be gathered from a single sperm whale. Mary Earle Gould (2) writes that "a candle made from spermaceti wax gave as much light as three tallow candles and a flame four times as large." The mid-eighteenth century found a number of Eastern coastal cities with street lights illuminated by spermaceti candles.

Tallow made from fat found near the kidneys of cattle was considered to be of the highest grade for use in making candles. Tallow makers used

A rectangular 36 tube tin mold used in the 19th century by itinerant chandlers or candlemakers who traveled the rural areas selling their wares. Collection Mr. & Mrs. John Curry.

a number of processes to obtain this substance. One common manner was to cut suet (hard, light fat found around the loin and kidney areas of cattle) into small pieces and heat it in large iron pots until the fat melted. It was then dried and the residue pressed until all the tallow was extracted from the tissue.

The most sought after substance for making candles undoubtedly was the bayberry or candleberry. Bayberry candles emit a fragrant aroma when lit, and burn quite slowly with little smoke. Miss Gould reported that bay-

Square 48 tube tin mold of the early 19th century. Some molds were made with as many as 120 tubes. Authors' collection.

berry picking reached such heights that laws were passed prohibiting the picking of the berries before a set date.

In his work, *The Ballad of William Sycamore*, Stephen Vincent Benet touched upon his dying character's lasting memory of early frontier living:

"And some remember a white starched lap,
And a ewer with silver handles,
But I remember a coonskin cap,
And the smell of bayberry candles."

The berry is found growing in clusters on the stem of the bayberry shrub *(Myrica pensylvanica)* which grows along the Atlantic coast and as far west as Louisiana. The berries were carefully picked, slowly boiled, and skimmed repeatedly until the wax took on a light green color. Bayberry candles were used only on special occasions and were expensive when purchased from a traveling candlemaker or chandler. The cost and relative scarcity of bayberry candles was due to the great amount of berries needed to make a single candle. A bushel of berries produces only four

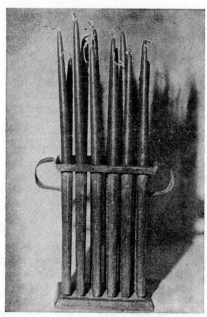

A rare 18 tube tin mold demonstrates its decorative possibilities when used as a candelabra; early 19th century. Authors' collection.

or five pounds of bayberry wax. Scientists today make use of the bark of the bayberry root in making a drug that shrinks tissue.

The productivity of the housewife-candlemaker was highly dependent upon the weather conditions outside her door. The months of September, October, and early November were considered the best time for molding candles. The fall months were advantageous for reasons other than the weather. Normally, cattle were butchered at this time and the tallow was readily available. A single candlemaking day could produce enough candles to light many a dank, dark winter's evening. It was possible for a housewife to make as many as four to five hundred candles in a day if she possessed a number of large molds.

The wicks used in making early candles were usually made from loosely spun cotton. Four to eight strands of the spun cotton were twisted together into a single wick. The greatest difficulty in molding candles was keeping the wicks taut within the tubes of the candlemold.

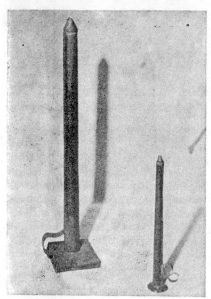

Left: Tin candlemold used to make large altar candles for churches; height 21". Right: Early 19th century single tube tin mold with fluted base; height 9½". Molds with 1, 2 or 3 tubes are more difficult to find. Authors' collection.

After the tallow was poured into the molds it took from a quarter to three-quarters of an hour to harden. When the candles were ready to be taken from the individual tubes the mold was dipped into a tub of hot water. The hot water loosened the tallow on the inside of each tube and the candles emerged from the mold unscathed.

After the candles were removed they were stored in the cellar of the home for from three days to a week. The candles were then stored in wooden, and later tin, candle boxes.

Bibliography

1. Christensen, Erwin. *The Index of American Design*. New York: Mac-Millan Company, 1950, p. 92.

2. Gould, Mary Earle. *Antique Tin and Tole Ware*. Rutland, Vermont: Charles E. Tuttle Company, 1958, p. 104.

3. Hayward, Arthur. *Colonial Lighting*. New York: Dover Publications, 1923 (revised 1962), p. 78.

4. Coffin, Margaret. *History and Folklore of American Country Tinware, 1700-1900*. Camden, N. J.: Thomas Nelson & Sons, 1968.

Hitching Weights

by F. M. GOSLING

FIG. 1

FIG. 2

THE IRON weights shown here were used in lieu of a hitching post or hitching rail in the days of the horse and buggy. A leather strap, approximately 4 feet long, with a snap attached to each end, was fastened to the weight by one of the snaps and the contrivance carried in the buggy. When no other means of tying the horse was available the driver lifted the weight by the strap, placed the weight in front of the horse, and snapped the other end of the strap to the bridle. A driver could leave any well behaved driving horse secured in this fashion and be reasonably sure the rig would be in the same location upon his return.

From time to time someone brings up the question, often with tongue in cheek, as to the correct name for these weights. Included in the answers will be "curb weights," "hitching weights" and "tether weights," not to mention what they were called when accidently dropped on someone's toe.

Perhaps hitching weights would fit them best. A search through 6 old hardware and mail order catalogs showed a listing in only one, a Montgomery Ward & Co. catalog of 1902-1903 in which they appear as "Hitching Weights, 16 lbs. price 50¢."

The top of Figure 1 reads "S H Co./12." Figure 2 bears the wording "N Lansberg & Son."

Oddities in Early American Tinware

by CARROLL HOPF

THE COLLECTOR of antiques has a wide choice from which to make his personal concentration. If, for example, he elects Folk Art as his interest, he may generalize and collect objects in such diverse media as iron, wood, pottery, or glass, or he may specialize in some particular category. The photographs here represent a specialization of artifacts fashioned from tinplate.

Tinwares are made of thin iron sheets coated with tin. The tin retarded rust and provided a bright, easy-to-clean, sanitary surface. By present day standards, the tinplate objects pictured here can be classified as oddities, or at least in the realm of the unusual, when compared to the ordinary everyday

This particular form of ear trumpet is advertised as the "Miss Greene Hearing Horn" in the 1901 Sears, Roebuck & Co. catalog. "Its peculiar formation is especially adapted to gather in sounds and convey them audibly and distinctly to the ear." It has a black japanned finish and measures 18¼" in length. **Collection of Miss M. Carrie.** (Photo by Poist)

The tin shaving mug is probably contemporary with pottery and porcelain examples which also bear an appendage to the side. It is interesting to note the variance in the appendages. Many are in circular shallow bowl form added at the top of the mug; in this form the lather was raised from soap. The other type of appendage, as shown here, was fitted onto the side and extends the height of the mug. This probably served as a storage receptacle for the shaving brush. Measuring 4¼" high and 3¼" diameter, this example dates from the last half of the 19th century. **Penna. Farm Museum Coll.**

"Mr. & Mrs. D. W. Van Auken, From Reform School" is inscribed on the crest rail of this delightful tin chair. A decorative twisted banding is applied to the top of the crest rail, center splat, and around the seat skirt. The chair has never been painted. Probably dating from the last quarter of the 19th century, it has an overall height of 35". **William Penn Memorial Museum Collection, Harrisburg ,Pa.** (Photo by Karl G. Rath)

utensils fashioned in tin over the years —the pails, dippers, measures, and canisters that were made in abundance.

All of these examples are products of local tinsmiths who, along with various other craftsmen, once formed an important segment of our rural society. In addition to being unusual in form, each piece reflects a high degree of skill and expertise of craftsmanship on the part of its maker.

Good tinware of high quality may still be found on today's antique market. Approximately half of the items illustrated were purchased within the past four years.

That our ancestors were a thrifty and saving lot is well attested by this pitcher, mended with a tin handle. The humble repair is ably done and expresses someone's skill as a worker of tinplate. The pitcher is an earthenware type quite common during the middle decades of the 19th century. It is banded in blue and white slip and of English origin; 8" high, 6" diameter. **Penna. Farm Museum Coll.**

Molds for puddings and jellies are found in a multitude of shapes and forms. A collection of the many forms is in itself a very rewarding effort. A horseshoe form, as this example, is probably scarce when compared to the frequency other shapes are found. It is 7 1/2" in length, 7 3/8" in width, and 2" deep; dating probably from the last half of the 19th century. **Penna. Farm Museum Coll.**

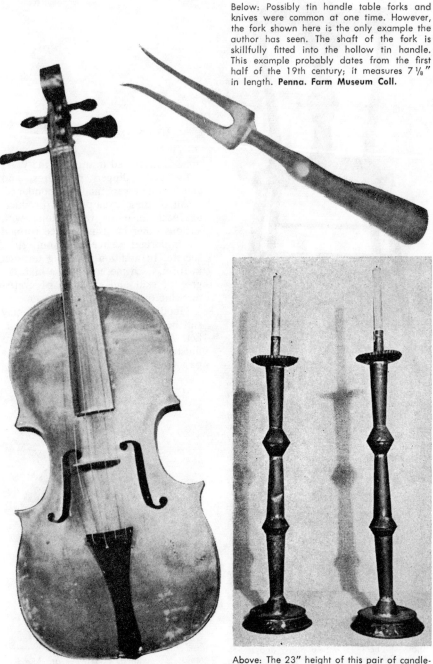

Below: Possibly tin handle table forks and knives were common at one time. However, the fork shown here is the only example the author has seen. The shaft of the fork is skillfully fitted into the hollow tin handle. This example probably dates from the first half of the 19th century; it measures 7 1/8 " in length. **Penna. Farm Museum Coll.**

Above : The tonal quality of this tin fiddle is admittedly not as fine as that of a wood fiddle. No pertinent information is known concerning this example—why it was made of tin, where it was made, or by whom. The perfect state of condition attests to its being well cared for through the years. Its length is 22". **Penna. Farm Museum Coll.**

Above: The 23" height of this pair of candlesticks makes one suspect they were made for use in a public building, perhaps a church. A good sense of design and proportion is exhibited in the interesting form of the shafts. The bases are sand filled. Dating from the first half of the 19th century, they were discovered in Berks County, Pennsylvania. **Author's Coll.**

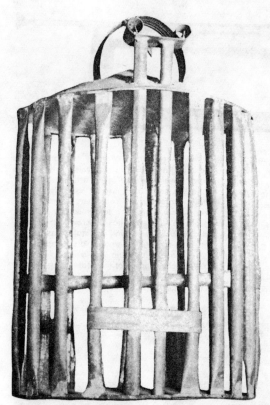

Of early 19th century origin, this bird cage may well have housed a quail, cardinal, robin, or any other bird small enough to fit in it. Completely made by hand, it has a sliding up and down door, two bars of which extend through the top of the cage. It is 13″ high; 9″ in diameter. It was discovered in central New York state. **Author's Collection.**

Below: Upon several occasions tinplate containers similar to the illustrated examples have been referred to in contemporary writings as ''measures.'' Certainly they may have served this purpose; however, their cylindrical form and side-mounted strap handles at the top are derivative of the drinking mug form used in the latter 18th and early 19th centuries. It may well be that they were used as drinking vessels. Respectively they measure 6″ and 9 5/8″ high by 4″ and 5″ diameter. Both probably date before mid-19th century. **Penna. Farm Museum Coll.**

Above: Tin Horns are generally common items. The majority are straight forms measuring anywhere from 12″ to over 4 ft. in length. They were used frequently by coach and stage drivers, peddlers, and on the farm to hail the men in from the fields. This example is unusual for its rectangular form. It emits a powerful one-note tone. Probably dating mid-19th century, it measures 23″ overall length. **Penna. Farm Museum Coll.**

Below: A genuine "Whatsit," this ambiguous looking tin object has puzzled all of the experts we consulted in an attempt to determine its name and use. It consists of two shallow disc-shaped containers connected by two hollow tubes. The larger container, 16¼ inches in diameter, has a screw cap closure, so obviously some kind of liquid was poured into this object; the smaller disc-shaped container has no opening. Its overall length is 26½ inches, and both containers are about 4 inches in depth. The author would welcome any suggestions about its use and origin.

Far right: Tin pipes would seem impractical for smoking tobacco, and it's quite possible that they were actually used by children to blow soap bubbles. Some people believe they were intended as tin anniversary gifts. Certainly very precise workmanship is revealed in its making. The example shown is 7 inches long, and was probably made in the last half of the 19th century.

Right, center: This tin Leader Box originates from the Mohawk Valley in upstate New York, and quite probably from the Fort Plain area.

Applied crimped banding and a star motif add extra interest to the overall form. There was at one time a quarter moon applied next to the star.

Leader Boxes originally served the functional purpose of connecting house gutters to downspouts. Their use explains why so few are found today; many have rusted to pieces right on the houses. This example probably dates from the second quarter of the 19th century. It measures 22″ high. **Privately owned.**

Left below: A tin kerosene lamp, circa 1870, exhibits construction features found in earlier whale oil and fluid burning lamps. Notably the sand filled base and the conical shape reservoir are reminiscent of earlier lamp forms. We cannot dismiss the idea that this lamp may have been converted from whale oil to kerosene. It stands 12″ high and measures 4¼″ in diameter around the base. **Penna. Farm Museum Coll.**

Kitchen Tinware

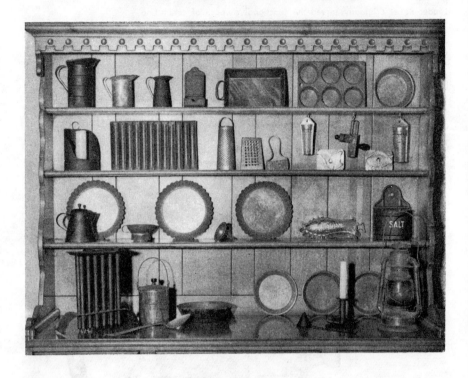

by LOUISE K. LANTZ

THE early nineteenth century cook, accustomed to kitchenware of cumbersome iron and heavy pottery, welcomed the advent of the tin-plated iron or steel called tinware. Quite literally, it lightened her work; today's thin weight products were beyond imagining. The tinware pictured here, from the author's collection, embraces a time span of nearly a hundred years, from hand-crafted pieces of the early 1800s to patented gadgets of 1911.

First on the top shelf are three sizes of measures, handmade, probably by the master of the house. The hanging wall match safe, so convenient to hold the many matches needed for oil lamps and coal or wood stoves, is factory made. These were produced in quantity and in wide variety of designs. Next are a heavy single-handled early bread pan, a muffin tin patented in 1874, and a small deep pie pan.

On the second shelf is a shielded candleholder, home-crafted, to be hung by its brass ring, or set solidly on its wide base. The breadstick pan makes 12 sticks; others may make 6, 8, or 10. The handled round vegetable grater is hand-punched, probably early nineteenth century; the factory-made grater beside it is of the same period. The handled chopper with corrugated blade is one of six different shapes in the author's collection. The three hanging graters are nutmeg graters. The center one, with wood knobs, was patented in 1896 and guaranteed not to "clog, tear the fingers, nor drop the nutmeg." (The nutmeg is held tight to the grater by a spring on the side, and is grated very fine, distributed evenly and entirely, leaving no waste.) The backed cookie cutters, in shape of duck and fish, are handmade. Many other intriguing shapes are to be found, with a hole or two for poking out the cut cookie.

The third shelf boasts three fluted-rim cake pans; a small coffee pot with heavy copper bottom; a funnel for filling canning jars; a smaller funnel advertising C. D. Kenny Co. (an old Maryland grocer); a fish-shaped aspic mold; and a hanging salt box.

Bottom Shelf

On the bottom shelf is a graceful 12-hole candlemold, from the collection of Mary Keefer. Next come a covered, bail-handled lard pail, and a deep heavy cake pan with tapering sides, sometimes called a corn pone pan. A well used stirring spoon is in front. The first of the three pie pans advertises the Baltimore Pie Bakery, last listed in City directories in 1911. In front is a tin candleholder, with an extinguisher near by, and a Dietz lantern. The lantern, commonly used outdoors and in the barn, was often handily hung by the kitchen door.

Other interesting old tin-plated kitchen articles to be found without great difficulty are tart and patty pans, tube cake pans, japanned bread boxes, rotary flour sifters, egg beaters, dippers, colanders, scoops, serrated-edge bread knives, spatulas, drip pans, doughnut cutters, fruit and vegetable presses, even dustpans!

The molds here pictured may be characterized as follows: *Top row:* Geometrical, swirl, cornear and pineapple, from J. & C. Berrian, c. 1848. The high molds are for ice cream. *Center row:* Lion top, fig cluster, ice cream column and sheaf of wheat. *Bottom:* Rose, pineapple, and grape molds. All the large molds here pictured are jelly molds, said to have been either imported or made by Stoughtenbaugh of Brooklyn, N.Y., mid-19th century. Actually, Yarnall of Philadelphia was selling the same type of molds in the 1840's.

Primitive Tin Graters and Strainers

Above: The two types are positioned for grating. *At left:* Reversed for use as strainers.

Two types of strainer-graters. One is box-like with pierced tin bottom; the other is a piece of pierced tin set in a plank.

by EDWIN C. WHITTEMORE

TWO OR three hundred years ago, household utensils in most of America were made of iron, pewter, or earthenware. Iron was heavy and brittle, and it rusted. Pewter was heavy and dentable, and it melted. Earthenware was bulky and heavy, and it broke. They were not ideal materials for items to be given hard use, in contact with cold liquids and hot fires.

It is easy to see why "tinware" was accepted so quickly, and became popular so very fast. Actually, the term "tinware" is a misnomer, for tinware, as we know it, is actually sheet iron on which layers of tin have been deposited. Often 85 percent of the total content is iron.

Tinware was developed in Germany in the 1500s, moved quickly to the British Isles where there were both rolling mills and a supply of tin ore. In England, tinplate, and tinware items made from it, were produced in the early 1600s. In the early 1700s, the American colonies started importing both finished tinware items and the rolled tinplate sheets from which to fabricate household utensils.

Tinware actually did not need much of a push for housewives accepted it willingly. It was shiny and sparkling, the "poor man's silver." It was light; it stood heat; it could easily be fashioned into many types of items. It was relatively inexpensive; it did not crack or melt; it resisted rust, and could easily be mended by soldering.

The special category of "pierced tin" housewares is one of the most interesting in the tinware field. Immediately we think of pie safes with pierced tin panels, foot warmers, lanterns, graters, colanders, and related items.

Usually the tinplate was pierced before the item was assembled. A sheet of tinplate of the required size was cut from a flat sheet and placed, still flat, on a suitable surface, such as a sheet of lead, a pine plank, or even hard wet sand, packed solid. Then, with a hammer and nail, or better, a hammer and sharp edged chisel, the worker pierced the sheet in various designs, simple or intricate.

If a nail was being used and hit-or-miss designs employed, the result was most varied. With a more skillful artisan, using a sharp chisel, the result could be quite delightful. Most often the piercings were slots or dots, but with special cutters, other design elements were incorporated, such as stars, half moons, and crosses. Related to piercing was the simpler "embossing," where patterns were accomplished without cutting completely through the tin.

Piercing was done in the tinplate for functional reasons as well as for design. In lighting devices such as lanterns, it let oxygen in, heat and smoke out. In graters, the rough side became the work side, the rough edges of the pierced holes doing the grating. As a strainer, the smooth side was a practical workable surface which provided drainage.

We show here two examples of an ingenious household device depending on pierced tinplate—the combination grater-strainer. Both sides of the tinplate are functional in the same piece. In the boxlike example, a sheet of pierced tinplate covers one whole side. Placed with the rough side up, it serves as an excellent grater for cabbage, carrots, and potatoes when they are being grated to make coleslaw, to color butter, and in making starch. Turned to the other side, it becomes an excellent strainer or colander of good capacity for washing vegetables and such.

The other example, made from a plank, is identical in function, but with smaller capacity, and probably represents a buried improvisation.

These combination grater-strainers are very collectible. They may be used for their original purpose, or simply hung on the wall for decorative effect. They may be wired with a low-wattage bulb to give a soft and patterned light in a special location, such as a hall or infant's room. They represent an interesting group of the "practical primitives" which are becoming more and more popular with collectors.

Tenth Wedding Anniversary Tinwares

by GLADYS REID HOLTON

Tin fans fashioned for 10th anniversary gifts. The larger is 17" long overall, 12⅝" in diameter; the smaller, 8" in diameter has a 15" long chain attached to the handle, designed to be hooked to milady's belt. Both fans show signs of use.

THE CUSTOM of "celebrating wedding anniversaries has of late years been largely practiced," wrote John H. Young in 1881 in *Our Deportment, On the Manners, Conduct and Dress of the Most Refined Society, Compiled from the latest reliable Authorities.* "They have become a very pleasant means of social reunion among the relatives and friends of both husband and wife. Often this is the only reason for celebrating them and the occasion is sometimes taken advantage of to give a large party of a more informal nature than could be given under other circumstances. The occasion becomes one of the memorable events in the life of the couple whose wedding anniversary is celebrated. It is an occasion for recalling the happy event which brought to each a new existence and changed the current of their lives. It is an occasion for them to receive congratulations upon their past married life and wishes for many additional years of wedded bliss. Upon this occasion the married couple sometimes appear in the costumes worn by them on their wedding day."

Ten years later, in 1891, Richard A. Wells, in *Culture and Dress of the Best Society,* was still extolling the celebration of wedding anniversaries as "one of the pleasant customs which is coming into general favor," and adds, "Special anniversaries are designated by special names indicating the presents suitable for each occasion."

For the tenth anniversary, designated as "Tin," he suggested: "The invitations for this anniversary may be made upon cards covered with tin foil or upon the ordinary wedding note paper with a tin card enclosed. Those guests who desire to accompany their congratulations with appropriate presents have the whole list of articles manufactured by the tinner from which to select.

"A general frolic is in order at the tin wedding. It is an occasion for getting together old friends after 10 years of married life. Gifts are usually in the form of kitchen utensils—tin candlesticks, tin fans, tin ornaments, even tin tables and chairs are offered as gifts. These cause much merriment as well as showing the ingenuity of the giver."

Today's 10th wedding celebration would be exciting if Mexican tinware were used for table settings and decorations.

Tin has been a valued metal since ancient times. The early Egyptians sought sources for tin in countries outside their borders. The inhabitants of Mesopotamia obtained their supply from mountains in the northern part of their own land. As the world widened, deposits of tin were found in the Balkans, Bohemia, Brittany, and northern Spain. Tin was found in England, in Cornwall, and some historians believe this was one of the

Folding fan, with 12 10-inch sticks and two guards of pricked tin, including the letter "B" in the design; mount of paper with watercolor paintings of two sailing ships.

Left: Tin flower vase, 8⅞" tall, 3½" diameter at top and base. Right: Tin bouquet or posy holder for carrying a corsage, 6½" long, 1¾" at the opening.

primary reasons the early Romans invaded and occupied that land.

In those early days tin was used primarily in the manufacture of bronze. By 2000 B.C. it was being smelted and refined, and eventually bars of more or less pure tin replaced raw tin ore as a trades goods.

In colonial America before there were rolling mills, sheet tin was imported from England. Sheet tin was made principally of iron, therefore subject to rust and corrosion. To preserve the metal, tinsmiths and dec-

Dressy tin comb for the hair, 6" long overall, 6" wide.

orators of tinwares painted their goods or used a finish known as "japanning," a technique which had come to America from the East via England. Japanning was achieved by applying several coats of asphaltum over the surface of the bright tin. One coat produced a thin, transparent, light-brown finish; additional coats resulted in a darker, more opaque finish.

Connecticut was one of the early centers for the training of tinsmiths. As the supply of tinplate increased, larger quantities of tinware were produced. On April 27, 1767, Benjamin

Marshall of Philadelphia advertised that he "produced plain, painted, japanned, and planish tinware." (Planishing is the light hammering of metal to produce a smooth surface.) In 1832, 11 shops in Stevens Plain, Maine, produced a total of $27,300 worth of tinware. Soon enough tinwares became "everyday common."

By the 1880s and 1890s when articles of tin were decreed as 10th wedding anniversary gifts, donors

Lined tin jewel box, 4½ x 3½", 1¾" deep.

went to great lengths to provide something "different," and ingenious tinsmiths seemed never to run out of ideas for fanciful handmade remembrances to "cause merriment."

Wedding Anniversaries

1st — Paper	7th — Woolen
2nd — Cotton	10th — Tin
3rd — Leather	15th — Crystal
4th — Books	20th — China
5th — Wood	25th — Silver
6th — Candy	50th — Gold
60th — Diamonds	

Painted Tinware, Pontypool, and Painted Toleware

by CARL DREPPERD

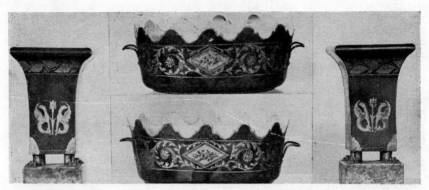

Pair of Directoire, painted tole jardinieres, in green and gold. Date is c. 1795, or perhaps as early as 1785. The square bases are marbleized, the flaring quadrangular vase-form painted with griffons, torches, and vine in gold. Between the jardinieres, a pair of scalloped edge plant pans of Charles X period, c. 1825.—Illustrations courtesy of Parke-Bernet Galleries.

Many Collectors have been Confused, and Understandably
So, Over the Accurate Nomenclature for Some Collectibles.
To Clarify One Group Which has Long Suffered Misnomers,
Here is the Actual Difference Between . . .

SOME months ago a commentator on things antique in a Metropolitan paper referred to common painted tinware as toleware. "The peddler's gift to collectors" was his phrase. This writer had confused the term "toleware" with "tinware," an error in nomenclature all too prevalent, but which in essence is comparable to confusing Dresden with Nippon, or Chippendale with Hitchcock. Like many other and more grievous errors in print this one, perhaps, was only a reflection of the error in the minds of most collectors in respect of the meaning of painted tin, and toleware.

Tole is a French word meaning *sheet iron* or, *plate of steel.* An item of tole is nothing more or less than an item made from sheet iron or sheet steel. If the item is tin plated, it is to be characterized as *tinned tole,* or *tinplated tole.* If the item is painted and decorated, it is *painted tole.* Since it is *painted tole* that is almost invariably meant when the term toleware is used, it would be well, first to study the genesis of this ware.

Painted tole is the result of an effort to make a decorative, nonbreakable ware imitative of enameled ware (enamel on copper or some other metal, as Cloisonne, or Limoges) and comparable to fine ceramics. Some of the finest examples were made during the age of its beginnings, the period of Louis XV. The objects made ranged in size from the minute to the gigantic; from snuff box to bath tub! Lamps, bowls, lavabos, candlesticks, boxes, trays, table tops, painted by the most accomplished fine artists of that day were made of sheet iron for the Royal, the Noble and the wealthy. The high place popularity of *painted tole* continued through the century 1750–1850. And so we find examples reflecting the styles of Louis XV, Louis XVI, the Directoire, The Empire, Charles X and Louis Phillipe. The painted tole of the last period was of course of Louis XV revival style; the style we call Victorian. It should be remembered for all time that painted tole was a luxury item. The sheet iron itself was cheap. Its fabrication into objects was the work of master smiths. Its painting, after the coating with many layers of ground, carefully rubbed and baked, was by artists like Louis David and Virgie Le Brun. It was sold in the Rue de la Paix . . . but never vended by peddlers. Of that we may be certain.

Pontypool ware is the English equivalent of painted tole. Pontypool is a town in Wales where iron was wrought into sheets and finally rolled. Here, also, sheet iron was first plated with tin by application of the molten silvery metal. But Pontypool ware could be either plain sheet iron, or tinned sheet iron in its first phase of being. What made it a ware rich and rare was its painting by accomplished artists of the stature of Angelica Kauffman, and Francesco Bartollozzi. Pontypool ware attained high vogue in England during the great classic revival staged by the Brothers Adam. It, too, was luxury ware of high price. Again, we may be sure, it was never peddled by itinerant vendors. Was it sold in the American Colonies? Was Painted Tole known and enjoyed here? Indeed yes. But in the homes of Royal governors and the mansions of the rich and well-to-do. No lane and by-way peddler ever had it for sale.

Painted tinware was the cheap imitation of painted tole and Pontypool. There is no cause for wonder about this. The imitation of luxuries, as cheap products, was a phenomenon in every field. Even the highly prized silver lustre ware of this day—as an antique—was once nothing more than the cheapest of imitation silver. In the case of painted tinware, (meaning painted tinplated sheet iron objects, or even untinned sheet iron) the imitation got cheaper and cheaper; the painting less and less imitative of painted tole and Pontypool. Finally it became a matter of quick striping and slap-dash. Yellow ochre took the place of gilding; the palette shrunk to black, green, yellow, red and blue.

As the cost of production dropped to pennies per object, this painted tin became a peddler's stock in trade, along with unpainted, tinned sheet iron ware and utensils. Since the peddlers wares when painted cost a bit more than plain tinned wares, resourceful people bought the plain and painted it themselves. Some of this ware is quite well painted. And now, to pile error upon error, some people call this home painted tinned sheet ironware folk art!

For those who desire to be fairly precise in their use of terms, these simple definitions should be helpful:

Painted tole, or toleware: To be applied only to French, fine painted sheet iron wares made as luxury items.

Pontypool ware, or Pontypool: To be applied only to English, fine painted sheet iron wares made as luxury items.

Painted tinware: To be applied only to cheap or good painted, tinned or plain sheet iron wares made for popular sale, or home painted.

Japanned in America

by JOHN C. VITALE

Among the more desirable items in japanned tinware are "Coffin" trays, which derive their macabre name from the shape of contemporary caskets. Top: Japanned Coffin tray with gilt decoration. Bottom: Japanned Coffin tray with Chinoiserie decoration in reds and browns on a bottle-green ground; border in gilt. Both ca. 1830. (Courtesy Cleveland Public Library.)

ALTHOUGH the early New England Yankee is frequently accused of having been exceptionally "Puritan" in his tastes, one of the first crafts to take root in the American Colonies was the highly decorative art of japanning. Consequently, today, during the period of rising interest in American culture, the term —*Japanned in America*—has become extremely popular. It describes a golden moment in the broad cultural panorama of American folk art.

Japanning, like so many early American art forms, first became popular in England. During the 18th century trade with the Orient was flourishing, and the English tea merchants, ever alert for a new item to lure the public, brought back a wealth of elaborately lacquered tea chests and metal trays from the mysterious Orient. Impressed by the beauty of the designs, English craftsmen immediately began imitating these wares. Instead of painstakingly applying countless layers of lacquer— as was the custom in the Orient—the English craftsmen speeded up the process by using an asphaltum varnish solution that could be applied in one layer. When heated, the asphaltum dried to a brownish-black, partially transparent and similar in tone to the Oriental lacquer.

In Pontypool and Birmingham, where the new craft first took hold, the term "japanning" was used to identify the art, stemming from the fact that these imitations looked as if they had been "made in Japan."

When it was introduced in America, "japanned" articles won instant favor. Those who could afford the luxury of imported japanned tinware welcomed the highly decorative pieces with their romantic Chinoiserie motifs. For a moment in history, the japanned tinware helped the New England housewife escape from her cocoon of innocence and isolation.

So popular was japanned tinware in the Colonies that the craft was destined to find a home in America. Boston became the first center for America's japanners with nine industrious craftsmen working at this trade. Such cities as Salem, Newport, and New York all had at least one japanner working in the area.

One of the earliest and most skilled

japanners in Boston was Nehemiah Partridge. During the 18th century, when it was customary to practice more than one trade simultaneously, Partridge operated a small apothecary shop in "Treamount" Street and practiced the relatively new art of japanning as a side line. In 1713 he announced in the Boston *News Letter* that he did "all types of japanning at reasonable rates." For years, Partridge, and his contemporaries in Boston—Ambrose Vincent, Joshua Roberts, Stephan Whiting, and Robert Davis—supplied the needs of the local housewife.

Unfortunately the art of japanning was a slow and laborious process, and each article had to be carefully prepared, then baked; two or three coats of asphaltum were often required to achieve an opaque and almost black effect. Consequently, although a constant market was available to the japanner, many died insolvent.

Despite the fact that japanning was far from a lucrative trade in early New England, its popularity continued to gain momentum. Many gentlewomen, charmed by the delightful qualities of japanned tinware and furniture, desired to learn the craft. To satisfy this need, teachers of the art came forward. One such teacher was Joseph Waghorne.

Long recognized as a skilled japanner in both England and Colonial America, Waghorne announced in the Boston *Gazette* in 1739 that he "would teach Ladies to Japan in the newest Method invented for that Purpose, which exceeds all other Japanning for Beauty." When sufficient interest had been aroused among the young ladies of Boston, the dashing Waghorne opened a school for japanning on Queen Street. Each of the artistic "scholars" were charged the sum of £5.

With the continued interest in the art of japanning it was inevitable that the craft would develop into a large scale business of manufacturing. The man destined to accomplish this goal was Edward Patterson. Patterson, a Scotch-Irish imigrant, who arrived in town with 18 cents, opened a factory for japanning tinware at Berlin, Connecticut in 1770. Long before, however, Patterson—aided by his brother William and his sister Anna—had begun working imported sheets of tin into cooking utensils at home, using wooden mallets. They first accumulated a stock, then sold it from door to door in Berlin and near-by settlements, carrying their wares on their backs.

Upon opening his factory, Patterson employed local women skilled in the craft. Although far from being as capable of matching the skilled work of the Oriental craftsmen, these women developed a forthright style of painting using both freehand methods and stenciling. Dynamic brush strokes and the use of bold primary colors became their identifying trade marks. The technique of japanning employed by Patterson's skilled women was basically simple. They began by working out designs in gold-leaf patterns. Next the design was painted in with clear varnish, or with lamp black and gold size. Baking the decoration to a hard finish was the last step.

Patterson's output of tea trays, pans, kettles, and every other kind of household tinware was prolific, but it was not until much later that mass production methods entered the field of decorated tinware. This feat was reserved by chance for Oliver Filley of Bloomfield, Connecticut.

Like Patterson, the industrious Filley began his career as a tinsmith and part time peddler. He was acquainted with everyone connected with the metal industry in the state of Connecticut. When the opportunity presented itself, he bought the patent rights to a machine designed for working tin. The price was $20. With such a machine at his disposal Filley's production of tinware far surpassed that of Edward Patterson. In a steady and endless stream, trays, toys, and a vast assortment of small, decorated tinwares poured from the Filley factory. All were charmingly japanned in bright colors.

Because of Filley's tremendous output it became necessary to find new markets for japanned tinware. To accomplish this the Yankee peddler was called into service. Known commonly as "Sam Slick from Pumpkin Creek," the walking peddler began carrying japanned tinware into the deepest parts of New England. Within a few years japanned wares became the fastest moving commodity carried by the Yankee peddler. Soon the names of Patterson and Filley were known far and wide. Consequently, the mark which they and the scores of other lesser lights in the field of japanning left upon the American scene was a lasting one.

20th Century Childrens' Tins

by ERNEST L. PETTIT

Fig. 1

Fig. 2

Fig. 3

A S SOON AS machinery to make tin cans was developed, between 1860–70—up to then they had been made tediously by hand—other tin containers, especially for food stuffs, came on the scene. Merchandisers discovered early that art work on the new tins helped sell the product they contained; that decorated containers had special appeal to children—youngsters like to play with them, keep little trinkets in them, gather berries in them, or use them for lunch boxes; and that what children clamored for, parents usually bought.

As new techniques in printing and stamping appeared, designs and decorations in tin containers advanced. A young visitor at the 1876 Centennial Exposition in Philadelphia might have spent his pennies for a half-pint tin pail of peanut butter, undecorated except for the embossed lettering which identified both the product and the place of purchase. By the 1890s, boys and girls were begging for the gay tin Schepps Cocoanut can, printed in glowing colors with a monkey-in-the-jungle scene. Since the bright tin was advertising on the grocer's shelf, the name of the product or its maker was never omitted in its decoration. Sometimes the can maker's name appeared in tiny letters close to the top or bottom rim. Without this line, exact identification of the tin maker is impossible.

Gradually pasteboard packaging took over, and fewer products were put out in tins. The many small factories which had been engaged in making or printing tins for local areas went out of business or were absorbed by larger companies.

Early tins for children are delightful to own, but not particularly easy to find today. The colorful tin containers manufactured in the first half of this century are more plentiful. Though less distinctive, being quantity-made, they can add time-span to a collection of earlier examples or form the nucleus for an engaging "late" collection.

The six tins pictured here, designed specifically for children, encompass the period from 1900 to 1944. Not all of these were made to hold a specific product. Produced in quantity by large companies, they went to stores which either filled them from stock, usually with confections of some sort, or sold them empty for Santa Claus or the Easter Bunny to fill at home.

Fig. 4

Fig. 5

Key to Illustrations

Fig. 1—Armour's VERIBEST Peanut Butter came in this pail-type tin featuring a bail handle. The lettering in blue and white; the Mother Goose characters are in natural colors; the background is orange. It is 3¼ inches high, 10¼ inches in circumference, and was manufactured by the Continental Can Company of Chicago, Illinois, ca. 1900.

Fig. 2—This octagon-shaped box, 2¼ inches high, 5½ inches long, and 4¼ inches wide, is illustrated on the top and sides with the story of The Three Little Pigs. The background shades from pink on the edges to white, with the figures in natural colors. It was made in Mansfield, England, by the Metal Box Company, Ltd. (B. W. & M. Branch), ca. 1930.

The forerunner of this company was established in the 1890s, and was known as the metal box making firm of Barringer, Wallis & Manners. In 1921, the union of this firm with Barclay & Fry and Hudson Scott produced the Allied Tin Box Makers, Ltd. In 1922, the firm name was changed to The Metal Box & Printing Industries. In 1930, the company be-

Fig. 6

came the Metal Box Company Ltd., and as such exists today.

Fig. 3—Oval in shape, this box is entitled on the cover "Peter Rabbit on Parade." In natural color, Peter Rabbit and his friends—Unc' Bill Possum, Herry Hop Frog, Sally Sparrow, Happy Jack Squirrel, and others —march around the sides of the tin. This box, 2¼ inches high, 12½ inches in circumference, was made by the Continental Can Company and carries the trade name of TINDECO.

Originally TINDECO was the trademark for the Tin Decorating Company of Baltimore, Maryland, a company owned by the American Tobacco Company for many years, and which manufactured tins for the packaging of that company's tobacco. When the American Tobacco Company sold TINDECO to Owens Illinois Glass Corporation, it became the Owens Illinois Can Company, a subsidiary of the glass corporation. In 1944 Owens Illinois Can Company (TINDECO) was sold to the Continental Can Company and is now Plant No. 9 of that corporation. The trademark TINDECO is no longer in use on its containers.

Figs. 4 and 5—Both of these are rectangular in shape, 2¼ inches high, 4½ inches long, 2½ inches wide. Both are Christmas tins and feature a carrying handle. *Fig. 4* has a red background with "Merry Christmas from Santa" printed on the cover. The Mother Goose characters are pictured in natural colors. Scenes on the sides are encircled by holly wreaths.

Fig. 5 has a blue background with "Twas the night before Christmas" printed on the lid. The front panel shows Santa arriving; the top has him climbing down the chimney; and the back pictures a fireplace with stockings hung waiting to receive him. Both of these could have been purchased with or without contents. Each has the trademark TINDECO stamped in the bottom panel. I am of the opinion these were made by the Owens Illinois Can Company, ca. 1930–40.

Fig. 6—This Circus Club Mallows tin is cylindrical in shape, 7 inches high, 9¼ inches in circumference. The caricature represents a circus baboon. He is attired in a bright yellow jacket, brown pants, red vest, white shirt with blue stripes, and a green necktie. The pull-off lid is his sporty yellow hat. There may have been similar tins made to represent other animals of the circus world. The Whittal Can Co. (non-existent since about 1930) made this tin, which originally held marshmallows, for the Harry Horne Company Limited (now Harry Horne Limited) of Toronto, Canada.

English Biscuit Tins

by HELEN McGOLDRICK

Fig. 1: *Bird's Nest* was enormously successful in 1908.

Fig. 2: *Golf Bag* celebrated the advent of women on the golf course.

> *Webster lists "Bis'cuit. 1. A kind of unraised bread, plain, sweet or fancy, formed into flat cakes and baked hard; commonly called 'cracker' in the United States."*

WHEN THE PRESTIGIOUS Victoria & Albert Museum in London sponsored a show of biscuit tins last Christmas, the imprimatur was finally put on this distinctive English manufacture as an important collectible in the decorative field. The 200 tins in that exhibition are a tiny portion of a collection that goes into the several thousands gathered and owned by an Anglo-American who wishes to remain anonymous.

Much of the information on biscuit tins—who designed them, how rights to them were reserved, etc., has been lost. Many of the biscuit companies have been subject to "take-overs" within the last five years, and records, along with thousands of old tins, have been destroyed in these amalgamations. So, as interest was growing in this country in biscuit tins as col-

Fig.3: Two of a large selection of bags that appeared over the years; *Fishing Creel* (left) and *Satchel* (right).

lectibles, the records of the names, dates, designers, quantities, etc., were being destroyed by the biscuit manufacturers themselves for "lack of space to house them."

Happily, the anonymous gentleman who owns the enormous collection has many of the facts in his files, among the most important being the proper names and dates of thousands of tins. Unwilling himself to capitalize on his collection, he has been most generous with time and information to make this article possible. His hope is that new collectors will interest themselves in the ways in which both the graphic design and the shapes of the tins reflected the artistic styles and the times in which they were issued.

Perhaps it all began back in the 1830s, when Thomas Huntley, a baker, offered his biscuits and buns to the passengers on the Bath to London coach when it stopped at the Crown Inn in Reading. So good were his wares, that travelers frequently wrote back asking that he send biscuits to them in other cities. To accommodate them, Thomas called on his brother, Joseph Huntley, a tinsmith and ironmonger, to make boxes in which the biscuits might be sent safely.

From this beginning grew two large fortunes and two world-famous businesses. Thomas' bakery became Huntley and Palmer; Joseph's tins turned into Huntley, Bourne and Stevens, tin box makers.

Actually, other manufacturers had

Fig. 4: *Bluebird* resembles a caricature and is actually more green than blue with a large red beak.

begun to sell their products in tins, and these boxes, whether for biscuits, tea, sugar, or whatever, had paper labels. In some cases a tin metal label was soldered on, but biscuits universally came with paper labels. As paper labels were often damaged by dampness, by rough handling on long journeys, or in the stores, the need was for a permanent way of indicating their contents.

In 1868 the joint efforts of the companies started by Thomas and Joseph Huntley achieved a milestone in packaging by introducing the first transfer printed tin (*Figure 8*). The process used was one patented by Ben George (Benjamin George George) of Hatton Garden. The design was by Owen Jones, an influential architect and designer of the time, who had a retainer from Huntley and Palmer for doing display cases and other design elements for their business. His first landmark tin had a design of arabesques and carried for the first time the Royal Warrant "By appointment to her Majesty the Queen." It is done in red, blue, and green.

Despite this great step in the elimination of paper labels, transfer printing could also suffer in shipping from serious movement of the cargo. Several years later, Barclay & Fry invented a direct method of printing on tin by offset lithography. Within another five years tins could be embossed and decorated with great elaboration. (Despite these advances, some paper

Fig. 5: *Greuze Tea Caddy* is one of many designs using famous paintings as a theme, in this instance Jean Baptiste Greuze's "Milkmaid" from the Louvre's collection.

labels were used well into the 20th century.)

From then on English biscuit tins had two purposes. The first, of course, was to protect the contents in shipping; the second, to lend both a decorative note to the furnishings of a home and a practical note since the empty containers could be used for

Fig. 6 , left: *Book* was copied from a 1704 edition of "Het Boek Der Gebede" in the British Museum's collection. **Right:** *Literature* was a single tin simulating eight books; such fake books were extremely popular in homes that contained only one real book—the family Bible.

Fig. 7: The romance of the rose covered *Log Cabin* and *Windmill* appealed to all but the sophisticate.

something other than biscuits. As years went on they served as sewing boxes, substitutes for clocks, candlesticks, picture frames, mantel ornaments, vases, fruit bowls, mirrors, toys and games, and repositories for all sorts of items.

Tins came in the form of Sevres vases, Louis XVI caskets, clock and candelabra sets, golf bags, cottages, windmills, binocular cases, handbags, fishing creels, false books, stacks of plates, and birds. They reflected the changing tastes of the times—from Owen Jones' opening arabesque through Chinese and Japanese motifs, Chippendale, the romanticism of Indian and Eastern settings, Art Nouveau, and Art Deco—with an overwhelming interest in the activities of the Royal family.

By the 1880s the tins could be shaped, embossed, and colored in elaborate style. In the 1880s and 1890s they became very elaborate, very ornate, and designs tended to be themes of current events, fashions, in a sense, of the year. There was no limit to the digressions from the cube or square permitted the unsung designers who worked for the tin manufacturers.

Generally speaking the tins are most interesting graphically and for their elaborate decoration up to 1900. Then began the period of imitating life. Tins looked like everything they were not. After World War I they began to be utilitarian; toys like "Perambulator" (*Figure 9*) or "Kitchen Range" for little girls; games such as Peek Frean's "Cocoanut Shies." Huntley & Palmer put out handkerchief boxes and an egg-stand in 1928. (Interestingly, only two designers' names are known out of the thousands of tins designed over this 60-year period, Owen Jones, and then, 60 years later, Mabel Lucie Atwell, the well-known English artist who worked under commission for Crawford & Sons in the 1930s.)

Biscuit tins were sold most widely during the Christmas season; being a double gift of food and an attractive container. They were largely bought as gifts by the middle economic class. The so-called Great Houses never had them; they were too small for the great quantities needed in such large households. Catalogs for the tins came out once a year—sent to the retailer by the biscuit company. (The biscuit company bought from the tin box maker.) The retailer chose the tins he sajnted and also specified the filling he desired in each tin.

The "Specialty" tin was the largest one offered. Then there were "Juveniles." This refers to size of tin, rather than to subject of design, and they were designated Juvenile 1, 2, 3, and 4. Miniature tins were made filled with "mechanical" biscuits, molded in shape, similar to animal crackers. Commemorative flat miniatures celebrated Royal weddings, birthdays, and Queen Victoria's Jubilee. The Lusitania, celebrated as a giant step forward in ship building, appeared in a miniature. The British Empire Exhibition of 1924, the Wormley Exhibition of 1924, the Prince of Wales' visit to India in 1920, the State Coach tin of Jacobs in 1937, the coronation of George VI and Elizabeth, the Silver Jubilee of George and Mary, the Exposition tin of 1900 of Huntley and Palmer, and the coronation tins for Edward in 1902, all were represented.

One of the most unusual tins is a miniature put out by Huntley and Palmer for the Paris Opera, containing a picture of the Opera on the tin. It was sold in the lobby of the Opera House and never anywhere else.

At the height of the craze for biscuit tins there were some 60 com-

Fig.10: *Grandfather Clock* is a very nice imitation in tin of much admired Chinese lacquered furniture; painted in black and gold with some little highlights of green and blue.

Fig. 8, right: The milestone tins issued in 1886 by Huntley & Palmer, the first to appear without a paper label and the first to carry the Royal Warrant. **Far left:** *Fireside* is decorated on four sides and the cover with Kate Greenaway figures.

Fig. 9: *Perambulator* with red haired baby appealed to grandmothers and children alike.

panies actually making biscuits, but there were 125 companies selling biscuits under their own name. The tin makers had competition for their wares and the most prestigious company would have the novel tin first. When they relinquished it, the rights would be sold to a second company. Thus the same tin could be used by many different companies. The famous little red trunks, for instance, were sold by 12 different manufacturers at various times, and we know that tea and sugar cubes were also sold in that same tin! The Sun Dial, used by Huntley and Palmer in 1893, was being used as late as 1928 by William Crawford & Sons.

Titles of tins would also reappear. For instance, the "Pheasant" was used in 1890 and again in the 1930s. Every tin has a correct title. Throughout decades of tin box manufacture, reproductions of famous paintings, reflecting the tastes of the period, were used.

By the 1930s the spiralling costs of manufacture caused the containers to be restrained in shape and design, and their appeal now rests in the gay colors and the wide range of subjects pictured on them.

Some notable tins, easily identified, with dates they were first issued:

Fireside (*Fig. 8*)—Huntley & Palmer, 1890

Polo (Polo and four other sports)—Huntley & Palmer, 1890

Carriage Clock—MacFarlane & Lang, 1899

Library—Huntley & Palmer, 1900

Literature (*Fig. 6*)—Huntley & Palmer, 1901

Picture Frame—MacKenzie & MacKenzie, 1903

Bagatelle (a game)—Jacobs, 1904

Plates—Huntley & Palmer, 1906

Bird's Nest (*Fig. 1*)—Maker unknown, 1908

Satchel (*Fig. 3*)—Maker unknown, 1908

Log Cabin (*Fig. 7*)—S. Henderson & Sons, 1910

Blue Bird (*Fig. 4*)—McVitie & Price, 1911

Golf Bag (*Fig. 2*)—Maker unknown, 1913

Camera (box type Brownie)—Maker unknown, 1913

Book (*Fig. 6*)—Huntley & Palmer, 1920

Windmill (*Fig. 7*)—Huntley & Palmer, 1924

Kitchen Range—Maker unknown, 1926

Egg Stand—Huntley & Palmer, 1928

Grandfather Clock (*Fig. 10*)—Huntley & Palmer, 1929

Perambulator (*Fig. 9*)—Huntley & Palmer, 1930

Coconut Shies (a game)—Peek Frean, 1931

Greuze Tea Caddy (*Fig. 5*)—Carr & Co., 1936

Walnut Tea Caddy—Wm. Crawford & Sons, 1937

Fishing Creel (*Fig. 3*)—Maker unknown, undated

Collecting Early Barbed Wire

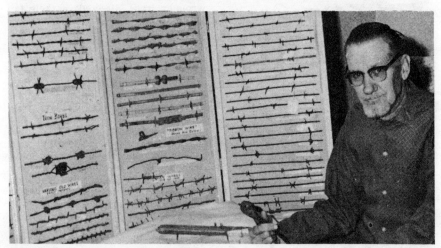

SINCE L. D. Martelle of Pierce, Nebraska, began collecting samples of barbed wire in 1940, he has found more than 250 different types. They have come from some 20 states and several foreign countries. But his collection is nowise complete, he says, for there were at least 400 different kinds of barbed wire made.

When he began his collecting, he was doing shelterbelt work with the Forest Service at Columbus, Nebraska. He had made a good start on his collection when he was sent to Haiti in 1943 to supervise the clearing of 3,000 acres of jungle land and the setting out of rubber plants. His choicest souvenir of Haiti was, of course, a piece of barbed wire! Back in Nebraska with the U. S. Department of Agriculture in soil conservation work, he continued his search.

"Why barbed wire? Mostly because it's a link to the past," says Mr. Martelle. "Barbed wire made it possible to settle the West. With barbed wire, the settlers for the first time were able to fence cattle adequately and eventually to turn to purebred livestock. The early samples are really something, but the inventors had the right idea."

LaSalle, Illinois, was the cradle of the early barbed wire boom, for there the idea for it was born when Julian Smith, in 1867, patented the first barbed wire. Though Mr. Smith's "spool wire" was never produced commercially, it led the way to other types which were.

Four principal manufacturers quickly sprang to action—P. T. Glidden, Charles F. Washburn, Isaac L. Ellwood, and Jacob Haish. Among the first types was the single wire with clamped-on barbs, the fencer doing the clamping. When Mr. Glidden brought out the two-strand twisted type, his competitors gave way. That is the only type manufactured today.

Two New York Makers of Early Tinware

by MARCIA RAY

Benham & Stoutenborough
Glen Cove, Long Island

IN TERMS of shop practice, the making of what is called tinware or tinned tole begins with the 18th century technique of hammering to shape over molds, anvils, and stakes, and reaches to the beginning of mass production when the "drop" process was used. This process, briefly, involved the use of heavy shaped drops of polished cast iron (sometimes wrought iron) directed in their fall upon a piece of the metal laid over a corresponding negative, or female, die.

The first objects made by E. Ketcham of Brooklyn, N. Y., by this process, were one-piece dairy bowls. (History of the firm indicates Charles Hodgett and William Taylor, practical tinsmiths, were among the founders, ca. 1850.) By 1865 they had perfected the technique to the point of making seamless tinware with sides varying only fifteen degrees from vertical. At that time Ketcham also developed the retinning process by which an extra coat of tin was added to the already tinned wares shaped in one piece, to cover all stresses, strains, and breaks in the original plating. Production was at high peak in 1876, with shipments

Illustrations of tinware from the catalog of Benham & Stoutenborough, ca. 1870, indicate the variety and excellence of their wares.

being made to all points in the United States, Mexico, and South America, and even to England and the Continent. Items of major antiques status produced by Ketcham are the planished wares which looked, originally, almost like silver, and the japanned wares, ornamented "in the very highest style of the art"—trays, coolers, toilet sets, and cake closets.

Andrews & Benham, tinsmiths, formed a partnership in 1840 at 111 John Street, New York, for the production of tinned tole and japanned tinned wares. When M. Stoutenborough, employed in 1846 as an apprentice, became a partner in 1860, the firm name changed to Benham & Stoutenborough. They moved to Glen Cove, Long Island, where they began *printing* decoration in colors on japanned wares with flexible blocks! Later they used lithography, applying the lithographed design on the sheets before forming into objects—substantially the same technique used today. Of high interest to collectors are their beautiful jelly molds, color-printed toilet wares, toilet stands, hand decorated coolers and water cans. Less well known are the tin tubes they made to hold nitro-glycerine, for use in the War between the States.

E. Ketcham
Brooklyn, New York

Oyster Dish.

Hip Bath.

Coffee Urn.   **Polished Teapot.**

Cake Closet.   **Well Bucket.**

Plate Warmer.

Chafing Dish.

Illustrations from E. Ketcham's catalog, ca. 1870, showing japanned and plain tinware for most every use.

Classic Examples of Early Tinplate and Tolewares— 1780 to 1840

by CARL DREPPERD

PERHAPS AT NO time in the history of collecting has tin-plated sheet iron, and plain or planished sheet iron ware (properly termed "tole" only when unpainted or unplated) been so popular with so many collectors. This, in turn, has resulted in the uncovering of many objects which, again in turn, pose a question as to their original purpose and use. In a broad scale research effort to determine, without question, the original names for such items, we have had exceedingly good fortune. We have found an illustrated catalog of such wares by a manufacturing exporter of England who had the rare good sense to designate every item he pictured, and to picture every item he produced. Thus the documentation is complete and unimpeachable.

This manufacturer, Tozer, of London (1780-1840), exported considerable ware to the United States, from the end of the Revolution. Here it became far more than a semi-luxury item sold in the more exclusive housewares stores; it became the prototype ware, the model ware, copied to some extent by every manufacturing tin and sheet iron smith (whitesmith) working from our earliest Federal era down to at least the 1880's. Many items became staples with our makers, a fact proved by comparing the price listings of Tozer with our American tinsmiths' price books and catalogs.

While the names given for the various objects shown here indicate their use, some require a bit of explaining: A Turbot pan was used to steam fish. A Batchelor's Broiler hooked onto a hob grate and was used to broil small birds, et cetera. A Breakfast Pot was a room service item—the pot proper for tea, the box-like cover for bacon, eggs, toast, et cetera. Candle Safes are candleholders, the candle burning within the pierced walls; it was also used to heat gruel, milk, or some other hot beverage.

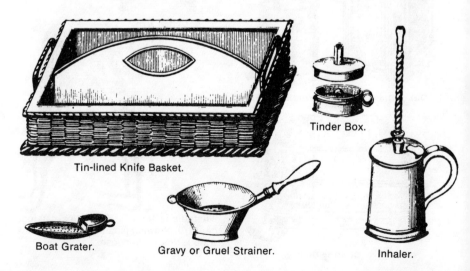

Tin-lined Knife Basket.

Tinder Box.

Boat Grater.

Gravy or Gruel Strainer.

Inhaler.

Hash Dish and
Burner.

Lantern with
horn windows.

Writing Candlestick.

Spice Box, round.

Oblong Tea
Kettle and Stand.

Cheese Toaster, planished.

Japanned Beer Jug.

Chocolate Pot.

Cheese Toaster for water.

Cheese Toaster.

Block Tin Stomach Warmer.

Oval Kettle.

Hanging Lamp.

Sugar Box, round.

Tea Cannister, square.

Large Candle Safe.

Bread Tin.

Sugar Box, square.

Oblong Dish Cover.

Bed Pan.

Ale Taster.

Spice Box, square.

Wine Mulling Pot.

Pannekin.

Treacle Can.

Milk Measure.